Which? Way to Repair and Restore Furniture

Consumers' Association
and Hodder & Stoughton

Which? Books are commissioned by The Association for Consumer Research and published by
Consumers' Association, 2 Marylebone Road, London NW1 4DX
and Hodder & Stoughton, 47 Bedford Square, London WC1B 3DP

Originally compiled by David Mason
Illustrations by Diagram Visual Information Ltd.
Designed by Libra Studios, Twickenham, Middlesex
Cover photograph by John Parker

First published, revised reprint 1983
Second reprint 1985
Third reprint 1986
Fourth reprint 1988
New edition September 1991

British Library Cataloguing in Publication Data
Mason, David
    Which? Way to Repair and Restore Furniture
    1. Furniture. Maintenance and repair
    I. Consumers' Association
    749.0288
    ISBN 0-340-55007-4

Thanks for choosing this book . . .

If you find it useful, we'd like to hear from you. Even if it doesn't live up to your
expectations or do the job you were expecting, we'd still like to know. Then
we can take your comments into account when preparing similar titles or,
indeed, the next edition of the book. Address your letter to: Publishing
Manager, Consumers' Association, FREEPOST, 2 Marylebone Road, London
NW1 4DX. We look forward to hearing from you.

Typeset by Tradespools, Frome, Somerset
Printed and bound in Great Britain by Jolly & Barber, Rugby, Warwickshire

Contents

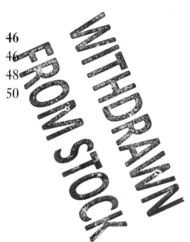

Introduction

This book is aimed mainly at meeting the needs of the home owner who takes an active interest in his or her furniture and is prepared to invest time and effort in preserving that furniture, or, alternatively, is setting up home on a budget and picking up second-hand items that, with a little care and attention, can be restored to useful life and good appearance.

This book adopts the working principle that there is a right way of carrying out a repair, and good cabinet-making practice applies to ordinary household furniture as well as to precious antiques. If the owner-restorer is prepared to invest a reasonable amount of time and effort in learning the skills involved, he or she will quickly find that it takes little more trouble to dismantle a faulty piece of furniture and reassemble it correctly than it does to carry out a botch job on it.

At the same time the book is not intended as an encyclopedia for the professional craftsman. To accumulate all the skills the essentials of which are described here, at a comprehensive professional level, a workman would have to serve a five-to-seven year apprenticeship in at least three trades – cabinet-making, polishing, and upholstery – and have some training in several subsidiary branches of those trades.

So this book is neither for the botcher nor for the professional, but for the home restorer. The householder will normally expect to work on only the few examples of each kind of furniture owned. Fortunately, providing he or she has the aptitude, patience and common sense, almost anybody can master the modest skills of basic carpentry and polishing that are needed for work on tables, chairs and cabinets.

Even for major renovations, involving stripping down, dismantling, reassembly and complete refinishing, the techniques required are only those employed in the average range of do-it-yourself household operations.

This book does not recommend that the home furniture restorer with a few hours' experience should start dismantling fine quality antiques.

But many people buy or inherit old furniture of a commoner sort which they could not afford to have restored at professional prices. For such owners, the techniques described in this book are exactly those that the professional restorer would employ. The only difference lies in experience, and it is therefore a recommendation throughout the book that any reader coming new to the work should start on simple household furniture on which mistakes will not be critical, or on pieces of junk furniture bought especially for practice. If you handle it, study it, take it apart, mend it and re-polish it, you will soon build up the necessary confidence and experience to carry out a wide range of repairs. With what you have learnt you can progress to more expensive furniture, confident that you can take the right steps to achieve the restoration that the article deserves.

For many people, the best source is close to home. Relations, retiring parents, close acquaintances, often own furniture in need of repair, without having the skill or the interest to restore it themselves. If you are lucky you may find something standing neglected in a corner, or hear of old furniture lying in pieces in an attic. Your practised eye will soon tell you the type of wood, the quality of the original workmanship, the finish it will have when restored.

The other main sources of furniture for restoration are the auction room and the junk shop.

In the auction room, you will have one great advantage over the dealers who will be bidding in competition with you. When they have bought the piece, they will have to pay a restorer to bring it to showroom condition, and add a substantial mark-up, to make the profit that will give them their living.

You have none of these problems. Once you have paid for the piece, you can restore it in your own time, at a minimal cost in materials. You can enjoy owning an article that might have cost you twice as much in a shop, and, as a bonus, can be certain of the quality of the restoration. ·

Junk shops are less predictable. In fact many of

them have disappeared, to re-emerge as antique shops with some pretensions to quality. The time when you could walk in and pick up a fine if dilapidated chair or table for a few pence has gone. Too many people are active in the antique and second-hand furniture trades to leave quality goods lying around with a low price mark waiting for the informed amateur to recognise their potential and scoop them up.

However, some knowledge of restoration will mean that you are able to form a reliable opinion about the type and extent of restoration a piece needs. Working on furniture, handling it, taking it apart, rebuilding it and refinishing it will give you knowledge that you could never glean from books or museums.

But furniture restoration needs a painstaking approach, and you may spend many an evening before a job is successfully completed. Almost inevitably, what starts out as an attempt to rescue a deteriorating article will become, in the search for structural soundness and quality of finish, an absorbing and time-consuming occupation.

And when you have learned something about the woodworking side of furniture restoration, you will have to learn an entirely new set of skills, in upholstery. If you work on one without the other, you will end up with either a set of chairs on which the wood looks perfect, but the padding a disgrace; or you may find you have a set of beautifully upholstered seats, on which the legs and other show-wood parts let down your achievements.

Fortunately upholstery, at least in the early stages, is not at all difficult, and it is possible for the beginner, working on simple seats, to carry out complete operations to a high standard without needing any special skills or aptitude.

The middle stages of upholstery, involving springing and sewing hard edges, appear to be intricate and complicated. In fact in this area, unlike cabinet work, the beginner can do little harm, as the results of his or her work are hidden inside the finished chair. The manual skills consist mainly of knocking in nails, tying knots and basic sewing with large needles.

In advanced upholstery complications may arise, but by that time you should have accumulated enough expertise to deal with them, and take pleasure in choosing from the vast range of materials, styles and trim that are available to enable you to design your own finishes.

But upholstery is also time-consuming and needs a steady build-up of experience. You should not expect to be building deep-buttoned chesterfields after a few evenings' practice.

People work at different paces, of course, but as a rough guide allow ten hours of work to complete a drop-in seat, two or three times as long to upholster a stuffed-over seat, and the equivalent of a good week of full-time work to build a small armchair.

When you start work yourself you will begin to appreciate why professional upholstery is so expensive.

In the long run, the great reward of this activity is a home full of well-kept furniture. Clean furniture, looking much as it did when it left its maker's workshop, but matured by time, is far more attractive than a piece in which years of grime conceal the character of the wood. A polish lovingly and skilfully applied by hand has more appeal than a manufacturer's sprayed-on cellulose finish, and a well-stuffed, well-trimmed armchair, in fresh, clean fabric, is more pleasant to use than a worn seat with its stuffing hanging out.

Beyond that, there is the further satisfaction of knowing that you have produced and maintained this furniture through your own effort and skill, without having to rely on the help of professionals.

For those readers who are interested in creating individual soft furnishings to complement their skills as furniture restorers, consult this guide's companion volume, *Which Way to Make Soft Furnishings*.

Conversion chart

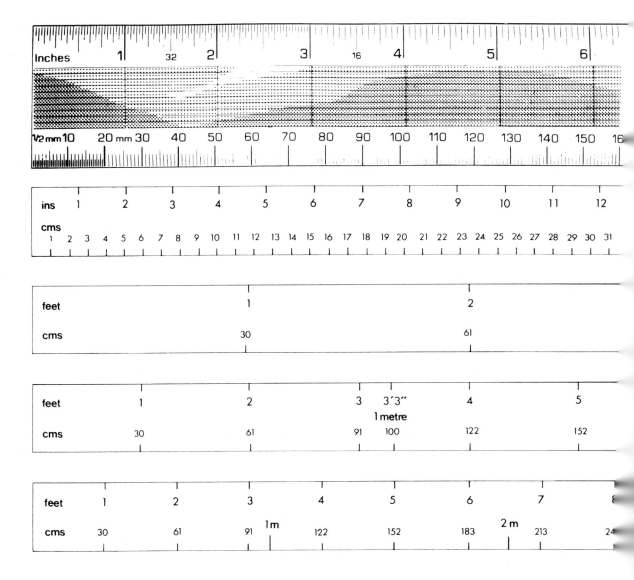

1 Starting

The first problem in almost all furniture repair is often the most difficult: identifying the piece and assessing what needs to be done.

Before you begin work, you will have to answer a whole series of questions about what attention the piece of furniture needs. You have to be able to tell what has gone wrong with it. You must judge how far it needs to be dismantled. You have to determine how much of the piece needs replacing, and how much you can preserve. If you do too much work you will have carried out not a restoration but a replacement; too little, and the faults you are trying to correct will show up again when the furniture has been in use for a short time.

Working on antique furniture, you have to be capable of restoring the piece in sympathy with the style and spirit of the original. If it is modern furniture – and some almost new pieces can be dramatically improved by the methods described in this book – you must be able to assess the details of its construction and finish, and determine which factory techniques could be improved by your own hand-work.

Many of these questions can only be answered in the light of experience and practice. There are no ground rules.

Watch how a skilled restorer approaches a job, and you will find that he first spends several minutes examining the piece. If you do the same, you will come to valuable conclusions that allow you to plan and complete a restoration effectively.

Feel the piece. Press your hands on it and move it about to test for firmness. Move the legs to see if the joints are sound. Run the drawers in and out to test for fit. If the piece is small, turn it over to look underneath. What sort of condition is it in? Can you see any woodworm holes? Are there signs of previous restoration? If so, how neatly was it done? If the furniture is large, kneel or lie down to look under it. If it is heavy and bulky, lean it back against a wall, protected by a duster or pad. Take out the drawers, turn them over and make the same kind of investigation.

Look inside the drawer recesses. If the runners are worn, will you have to replace them? Or can you just add a small piece of new wood?

This kind of investigation will give you a clear idea of the true condition of the piece, something often disguised by surface appearances. A few simple steps will enable you to assess a job.

Your knowledge of how furniture is made, gained from dismantling, reassembling and refinishing your first few pieces, will serve as an increasingly reliable guide in assessing the value of other pieces. If you are interested in going to the lengths of repairing and restoring your own furniture, you will soon find that your interest extends to collecting better, more attractive, and no doubt more valuable pieces.

There are no special difficulties. Anyone who can achieve average competence with tools can repair furniture. Manual skill is important, but even more vital is the right attitude. This kind of work requires monumental patience without which it would be wise not to embark on furniture restoration. Otherwise, it is simply a question of deciding where to start.

You will not choose a fine quality antique to begin learning about furniture repair: much fine furniture has been ruined by an excess of ambition over ability.

Start on an item of household furniture. Follow through the basic processes involved in repairing an ordinary chair, table, or chest of drawers, and you will soon know whether you have the patience and ability to work on more valuable possessions.

You will also discover that no two jobs are alike. Materials, construction and finish are peculiar to each item, and much of the satisfaction of restoration work lies in making decisions about how to deal with each case, and in knowing, from the appearance and serviceability of the restored article, that your decisions were right. As you begin to work on unusual and complicated furniture, you will find you have to devise your own techniques for restoration and repair.

But before you reach that stage, there are a number of typical processes to master. In each of the two main aspects of furniture work – woodwork repairs and upholstery – there are straightforward jobs that need doing in almost every home.

If anybody starting furniture restoration first carries out these simple projects, it will give them the confidence to move easily to the next stage. Often, each new process is only a small step in advance of what you have done before; sometimes, especially in upholstery, the work is the same, and the scale alone makes it more complicated. Even advanced work that would be formidable for a beginner appears simple if you have worked up to it by stages. Set yourself an informal 'course' on the lines which this book follows, and you should eventually accumulate skill and knowledge.

The rewards of furniture restoration are enormous. Often you can carry out work which would be too expensive to contemplate giving to a professional, and thereby save furniture you might otherwise have to scrap.

Once you have mastered the techniques of repairing the furniture, there is no reason why you should not go on confidently to make your own. The cost of quality hand-made furniture puts it out of reach of all but the wealthy, while the cost of materials is, by comparison, modest.

But the greatest rewards are the most intangible. The pride that comes from personal achievement, from being independent of other people's skills, is a reward that cannot be measured in money.

TOOLS

Furniture restorers need few special tools. Some experts prefer to work with smaller, lighter tools than are used in the average run of carpentry work, but ordinary household tools are adequate for virtually all the jobs you are likely to encounter.

However, if you are contemplating new equipment, you should consider your buying policy carefully. Tools are expensive, but providing you are going to use them on a regular basis over a fairly long period, they represent an investment.

Start with the smallest possible number but of the highest quality you can afford. Add a new tool to your collection when you need it, always buying the best you can afford. Before long you will find you have a comprehensive collection; the satisfaction of building up a tool kit seems to match the satisfaction of building the furniture itself.

Details of some essential tools are given in this book as their applications arise, but in general those that most restorers use are as follows:

Mallet
The cabinet-maker's model is smaller than the standard carpentry model, but either will do. Use it with softwood pads, in dismantling and reassembling.

Cramps
Essential for control of any work. Wedges and tourniquets can provide a substitute (see page 20). Buy two sash cramps at least 90cm long (you can make your own bars, as described on page 20), and two G-cramps, at least 10cm size.

Screwdrivers
Cabinet-makers' screwdrivers differ from engineers', being square ended and rather thick. They are produced in various sizes. The aim is to get maximum torque with the least chance of slipping, which can seriously damage surrounding wood. The better toolmakers supply screwdrivers with boxwood and beechwood handles, which seem more appropriate for furniture work than plastic-handled screwdrivers.

Start collecting a range, so that you can always find one which fits exactly the screw you are turning. That produces the best torque, and avoids stripping the metal from the screw. A medium (30cm) screwdriver is a good start, followed by smaller and larger versions as you need them.

Cruciform head screwdrivers are not yet generally accepted in quality cabinet work.

Saws
Most of the straight cuts in restoration work are possible using a tenon saw. Again, a smaller-than-average version will be more suitable for this kind of work. If you want to extend your range, a dovetail saw is an excellent supplement and makes a finer cut.

A panel saw is used for rough cuts and can be used for cutting along planks, though restorers normally buy wood cut roughly to size. Amateur restorers have no need of the full range of saws a professional carpenter would carry.

Planes

Today's planes are almost universally of steel, and will give greater accuracy than old wooden ones. A no 4 will serve most needs. In strong hands a larger plane will do all the same jobs and can be steadier because of the extra weight and length. However, it is more tiring to use.

Small planes are helpful for working with one hand in awkward locations on assembled furniture. The block plane is an example. Buy it when you need it.

Good suppliers also sell a variety for highly sophisticated work – plough planes, rebating planes, planes to cut mouldings. Generally, they are more useful in making new furniture from scratch than in restoration work. But if you are an enthusiast, you will soon find applications for them, and they make ideal presents. Study catalogues to decide on suitable versions.

Spokeshave

Closely related to the plane, it is invaluable for smoothing wood on curves.

Try-square

Essential before achieving very much restoration work. Bigger ones give greater accuracy but are more difficult to handle.

Mortice gauge

Gauges have one scribing point; mortice gauges have two, but can be used easily with only one. The largest version of this brass-and-wood tool produces the best work.

Knives

Surgeons' scalpels with disposable blades are extremely sharp but flexible. You will find them useful for a great deal of furniture work. A craft knife such as the Stanley knife is rather more robust, with a sturdy handle and stiffer blade.

Rulers

A flexible steel rule is very useful but not for closely accurate cabinet-work as it is unstable to handle. Instead, choose either a wooden rule (folding varieties are recommended) or a 30cm steel rule. The latter also provides an accurate and firm cutting edge.

Hammers

Rarely used in fine furniture work. Their main use is for hammering veneer pins, and for this a lightweight type is best.

Other tools

Pliers and pincers, to be bought as needed, a fret-saw for some veneer work, a drill and a brace, both with bits of various sizes are all helpful additions. A screwdriver-shaped bit is also useful, used in a brace for moving stubborn screws. Various bradawls, rasps and files may prove handy for particular jobs.

Power tools

They can save a great deal of work. The main ones are a power drill, which in inexperienced hands can give a more accurate hole than a hand drill, and various types of power saw. A circular saw, used by hand or on a bench, can make short work of long cuts. The more modern development, which some carpenters find indispensable, is the hand-held jig-saw. A supply of fresh sharp blades is relatively inexpensive and they are made in various grades to cope with different kinds of work.

Bench jig-saws and band-saws give excellent results, but are for the serious woodwork enthusiast interested in building up workshop facilities. Lathes also come into this category. If you are at the level where you want to use a lathe, you will know enough about woodworking generally to be able to choose and use the one you want.

Chisels

Rather than splash out on power tools, most amateurs would benefit by stocking their workshops with a good range of chisels, possibly the woodworker's and restorer's most important tools. A large proportion of restoration work consists of cutting away wood, replacing it, then paring that wood down to blend with other surfaces. Much of the rest consists of wood carving. Every article of furniture includes some joints and most of them need to be cut or at least cleaned with a chisel.

There are different kinds for different jobs, and different widths of chisel within each different type. You can manage with a limited number, but work is far easier if you can pick up the right one for the job in hand. This is one time where buying individual items may not pay, and it can be good policy to buy them in boxed sets.

However, the skill with which you use them is far more important than the type of chisel you buy. Given a choice, most restorers would opt for boxwood-handled chisels. As with screwdrivers, wood seems to come more comfortably to hand when you are working on fine furniture. The only drawback is that when you are using the chisel in any application that requires it to be struck, you will have to use a mallet. On a plastic handle you can use a hammer without damaging it.

The chisels most commonly chosen today for cutting joints are bevel-edged chisels. In amateur hands, these blades hold a sharp corner more easily than the older square-ended type: 6mm, 13mm and 25mm are probably the least you should have if you are intending to do serious restoration work of any kind.

On many joints a sash mortice-chisel is useful. Its blade is thicker from front to back than from side to side. This gives it greater rigidity and strength for cutting across the grain in mortices. Again, a small range of these chisels will prove invaluable.

SHARPENING CHISELS AND PLANES

Make a habit of sharpening tools ready for use, rather than waiting to find they will not do the job in hand.

You will need one oilstone, preferably two, a medium grade and a fine grade. If you can afford a coarse grinding stone too, it can be useful, but grinding the chisel is a job that rarely needs to be done, and you could reasonably leave that to a professional. Most woodworkers make up small boxes to hold their oilstones. The box keeps the bench and stone tidy, and with a top on, stops the surface accumulating dust and grit. You will also need a small can of household oil.

First secure the medium-grade oilstone on

your bench and squirt liberally with oil. Lay the chisel on it, pointing away from you, with its bevel edge facing downwards. Raise and lower the chisel handle until you can feel the bevel lying flat on the stone. If you rock it slightly you should feel a soft clunk as one end of the bevel then the other strikes the stone in turn.

When you can feel it lying flat, press the fingers of your left hand down to maintain the bevel in that position, and hold the chisel in your right hand (vice versa for left-handed people). Holding your right hand palm up, cradling the handle may help.

Now rock your body back and forth gently, so that your elbows start to swing. The chisel will move back and forth on the oilstone, and all the time your left hand will be holding the bevel flat against the stone.

Do this for a few seconds, then lift the chisel carefully, wipe off the oil, and check that you have smoothed out the bevel edge. If you have had reason to regrind your chisel, this bevel should be at 30 degrees to the flat face [1.1].

Look at the chisel again. You will see that right at the end there is another small bevel, probably about 2mm wide. This gives you the sharp edge. It should be at 45 degrees to the face of the chisel.

To hone this edge, place the chisel back on the stone, and feel again for the bevel you have just made. When you can feel it flat on the stone, raise your right hand sufficiently to lift the chisel on to the smaller bevel edge.

Now swing your elbows again. This time it is more difficult. The bevel is not long enough to feel and you will have to keep it flat simply by co-ordinating your body movements to keep the chisel moving in the same attitude. Avoid any tendency to roll the chisel on its edge, or from side to side. Either will destroy the edge altogether. Do this firmly and methodically for a dozen strokes, then take the chisel carefully from the stone and wipe off the oil. You should have two smooth and shining bevels.

Next feel the edge with your thumb, both sides. The side that was uppermost as you worked will have a distinctly rough feel to it. This is the burr, caused by the edge being turned over in your sharpening action. To remove it, go back to the oilstone. Rest the flat face of the blade on one edge of the stone, then gently raise the handle

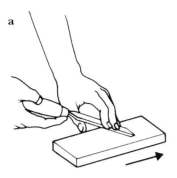

1.1a To sharpen a chisel, feel the bevel flat against the oiled stone, then move it steadily backwards and forwards.

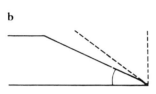

b The chisel should be ground and honed to give two angles, at 30 degrees and 45 degrees to the face.

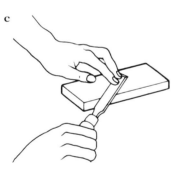

c Turn the chisel over, lower the face on to the stone, and rub it lightly to remove the burr.

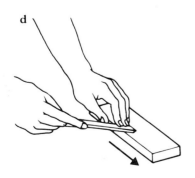

d Inexperienced workers might find it easier to sharpen the chisel with side-to-side movements along the stone.

and lower the blade, until the flat face comes into full contact with the face of the stone. Now draw the chisel towards you. Repeat the action. Do not jab the chisel into the stone or you will wreck your new edge. Just lay it down gently and draw it back. This will be enough to take off the burr, or at least loosen it, and you can carefully wipe away the fragments of metal on your palm. Some workers 'strop' the honed edge on the heel of their hand to remove the remnants of the burr. It is not a practice to be recommended to the inexperienced.

If you test the edge now you should be quite impressed. It will feel smooth and sharp, and you will be confident that you could work the toughest woods with it. But there is one more stage to go. Take out your fine-grade stone, apply oil to it, and repeat the entire procedure. Then you will have a really hard, compacted, sharp edge on the chisel.

Look after that edge. Do not leave the chisel lying on the bench. Not only is it capable of cutting you but if you catch it with another metal tool you will knock teeth out of it and will have to get the chisel re-ground.

If you can perfect the honing process, you will add a new dimension to your pleasure in furniture restoring and you will produce work of a consistently higher standard than you ever achieve with badly cared-for tools.

The most difficult part of sharpening is keeping the chisel at the same angle throughout. Practise this method because it is the correct way to do it, but if you really cannot achieve it, try turning the chisel through 90 degrees. You may find it easier to maintain the angle if you push it sideways and back, rather than back and forth along its length.

When the edge on the blade of your plane becomes dull, sharpen it in the same way. You will have to use a perfectly flat oilstone for this. So always, when sharpening a chisel, vary the area on which you work. Otherwise you will wear a pronounced valley down the middle of the stone and it will be useless for honing the wide blade of a plane.

If you buy a new plane, consider the type with disposable blades. Purists often frown on such developments, but many woodworkers are already won over. The supply of blades is not expensive, unless you are doing vast amounts of planing, and you will start each blade with a perfectly formed and perfectly sharpened edge. Their appeal lies especially with the mobile carpenter, who does not then have to worry about a blade going dull during a day's work and can save himself having to carry the weight of a spare plane or stone. But amateurs, even when working in the same workshop all the time, may still consider disposable blades a welcome time-saver.

There is one more tool that will need your attention. The cabinet-maker's scraper is a small rectangle of silver steel used for taking off unwanted old finishes, or very thin shavings from surface wood. Its use is explained in chapter 3.

Working with it dulls the edge, and you will have to restore it to effective working order. The process is almost opposite to honing a chisel. The edge on a scraper is bent over to form a T-shape [1.2c], which you use as a hook. Re-sharpening it is a three-stage process.

First lay the scraper down with its edge near to, but not over, the edge of the bench. Hold it firmly in place with the knuckles of your left hand (if you are right handed). You will now need a round steel tool, such as a strong screwdriver blade. With the steel shaft, 'strop' the edge of the scraper back and forth a few times to flatten out the hook of the 'T'. Turn the scraper over and strop the other side, then turn the scraper round and strop both opposite edges, to give you four scraping surfaces altogether.

Now take the scraper to the oilstone, hold it firmly upright, and work it backwards and forwards a few times [1.2a]. This will flatten out any irregularities and will also remove the flimsy part of the stropped-over edges, giving good firm corners to the hooks you are about to form.

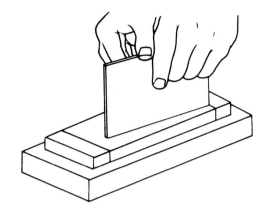

1.2a   After 'stropping' the previous edge down, square off the cabinet scraper edge on a coarse stone, with forward and back movements.

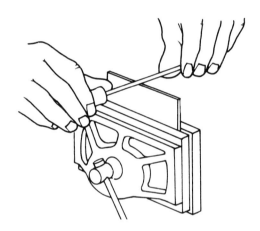

b   Draw a hard steel tool rapidly along the scraper to turn the edge again.

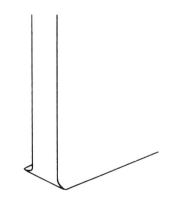

c   The new edge should resemble a 'T'.

Clamp the scraper in a vice and stand at one end of it. Take up the hardened steel edge used for stropping and hold it at the far corner of the scraper, precisely horizontally and at right angles to the scraper. Hold it firmly against the scraper's edge and draw briskly towards you. It will set the scraper vibrating and ringing. Repeat three or four times. Then turn the scraper over and do the same to the other edge. [1.2b].

Now feel the scraper with your thumb and forefinger. On both sides of its two long edges you should be able to feel a distinct hook, strong enough to catch the skin slightly as you pull your fingers across it. It will be perfect for working on the surface of a piece of furniture without removing the quantities of wood that a plane removes,

and without leaving the scratch marks that some glasspaper produces.

Looking after tools

They must be kept clean and wiped over occasionally with a lightly oiled rag to prevent them from rusting. They should be stored where they will neither be damaged nor cause damage.

Hang chisels, screwdrivers, hammers and other small tools in racks. The simplest type is a shelf with holes drilled into it of the appropriate size, and channels cut from the edge to the hole so that you can slip the tool through. It is noticeable how little space tools take up if held in this way.

Larger tools like planes should be placed carefully on their sides to protect the blades.

2 Structural repairs

The most vulnerable points in a chair are the joints where the side rails meet the back post. Every time someone leans back in the chair these two joints come under stress. Inconsiderate people often lean back so far that they lift the front legs off the floor. Then the load on these joints can amount to hundreds of pounds. Before long the glue breaks down and the joint starts to work loose. The chair is especially vulnerable if there are no bottom stretchers to help hold the frame square. Repairing an ordinary kitchen or dining chair is an excellent start to furniture renovation.

Examine all your chairs closely. Wobble the legs and back of each one. If the chair creaks noisily, or if you can feel or see 'play' in the joint, it needs repairing.

It may be possible to pull the joint apart slightly, work glue into the gaps you have opened, then cramp up the chair until the glue sets. But that is an unrewarding short cut. It is better to do the job properly, dismantling the chair, at least partially, cleaning away the old glue and re-glueing the chair correctly.

DISMANTLING A CHAIR

It is generally advisable to dismantle completely and put the chair in good order throughout, rather than make a partial repair and find you have to return to the piece because you overlooked a fault that had already begun to develop.

Chair parts are rarely uniform. Even corresponding rails on opposite sides can be cut to slightly different sizes, so trying to reassemble the chair from a pile of unmarked parts can be very frustrating.

Mark each piece clearly but inconspicuously, because you may later have to wash, sand down, or even plane away some wood, and pencil marks alone are not enough. Cabinet-makers would be horrified to see a ball-point pen used on furniture, but it makes a clear and almost indelible mark. Best of all is to make a firm scratch in the wood with a sharp pointed tool, or even cut a groove with a chisel, then fill in the mark with a pencil. Mark the underside of each piece (member), so that your signs will be out of sight on the reassembled piece. Mark all corner blocks, side rails, front rails – everything that would lead to confusion if you could not identify it.

Some workers use notches – one notch on all the pieces that fit together at one corner, two notches at another corner, and so on. Others inscribe letters on the wood, *rhf* for right-hand-front, for example. You will soon work out how far you need to take your own identification system, but in the early stages, be generous with marks.

At the same time, you will find a notebook useful for recording when you carried out the repair, how long it took, the cost, and what work you did. At the very least, a sketch of the piece and a note of how you marked it can prove invaluable when you come to reassembly.

When you have marked the chair, remove all the corner blocks. They may come free as you take out the screws. If so, wash off the old glue with hot water and put the blocks aside to dry naturally. If they remain glued in place, wait until you are ready to free the joint itself, then loosen the blocks at the same time by one of the methods described below.

Broadly, two kinds of joints are used in chairs. Good quality chairs generally have mortice-and-tenon joints. Less well constructed chairs, and many machine-made modern ones, have dowel joints, with either two or three dowels for each.

The mortice-and-tenon, especially in early chairs, may also be held by a peg let in through the tail of the tenon and glued in place [2.1].

Removing pegs
Remove them from all loose joints and any others you plan to dismantle. If there is some suspicion that the joint is being held firm by the peg itself, rather than by the structural strength of the joint, remove it.

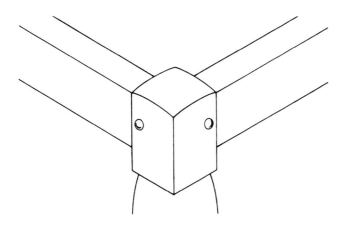

2.1 Joints in old chairs are frequently held by a peg through the mortice-and-tenon.

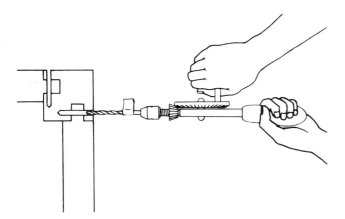

2.2 Tape the drill bit to clear the hole in the tenon, and drill out the centre of the peg.

First, take a sharp chisel and pare off the head flush with the surrounding wood. Now, with a small bit (3mm) drill a pilot-hole down into the peg. Next take a larger bit, smaller in diameter than the peg itself, but large enough to remove most of it without damaging the surrounding wood.

To discover how far down to drill, hold the drill bit against the outside of the joint, with the end level with the far side of the member bearing the tenon. Wrap a short length of masking tape round the bit, at the surface of the mortice-bearing member. Drill into the peg until the tape touches the wood. You can then be certain that you have cleared the tenon [**2.2**].

Next you will need a sharp narrow-ended tool. (You may have to make it yourself – all craftsmen gradually develop a range of gadgets which they have designed and made themselves for specific unusual jobs.) This one can be simply a small screwdriver, or a bradawl, with the end ground down to form a sharp chisel. Carefully cut away the sleeve of wood which remains on the inside of the hole after drilling. This process will clear the remnants of the old peg out of the hole, leaving the surrounding wood intact.

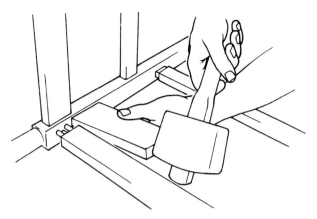

2.3   Hold a softwood block against the furniture and tap it gently with a mallet to aid dismantling.

Freeing the joint

It should now be possible to draw the tenon cleanly out of the mortice. But joints are rarely entirely clean, and swelling and shrinkage, combined with fragments of old dried glue, help to jam them.

To free a jammed joint, hold a block of softwood against the mortice-bearing part as close to the joint as possible, and tap it sharply with a mallet [2.3]. Do not be tempted to insert a chisel or screwdriver into the gap, you will only damage the wood. Also avoid putting any 'bending' stress on the tenon. Tap at each side of the joint alternately. And when dismantling the chair, work on the right and left sides alternately, so that the rails come out in parallel.

If a sharp tap does not free the joints, it probably means that fragments of dried glue have wedged it firmly in place. If the original cabinet-maker and any previous restorers have Scotch glue, you can free this easily by applying moist heat. It may be possible to soak a front corner joint for a few minutes in a bowl of hot water. To loosen joints in the chair back and other inaccessible places, hold the joint in the steam from the spout of a kettle. Alternatively, wrap a hot damp pad round the joint for a few minutes.

With any of these methods, providing old-fashioned woodworking glue was used, the glue should quickly soften and the joint come free. If the chair was assembled with PVA or other water-resistant glue, freeing it will be more difficult. Persevere. Eventually you will soften the glue, even if you have to soak the joint in hot water for several days.

Once the chair is in pieces, remove every spot of old glue from all the joints. Chip off any remaining large pieces with a chisel, then immerse the joint in a bowl of hot water, or hold under a running hot tap, until the glue softens enough to be wiped away with a rag.

Washing the parts should also clean off all the dust that has crept into the mortice, and any grime that has accumulated in the corners. If dirt still remains, set to work with a stiff brush or scrape it away with a sharp knife or chisel.

Treat both the mortice and tenon, and the male and female parts of a dowel joint, to the same scrupulous cleaning process, then let all the wood dry out naturally.

If you have chosen a chair where the only problem was loose joints, you can begin reassembly at once. But it is likely that the dismantling operation will have revealed several other faults. Legs may have split under the pressure of dowels. Part of the tenon may have split away so that you cannot achieve a firm joint without inserting new wood. The back rail, or upright, may be split, in which case you will have to carry out serious structural repairs before you can contemplate putting the chair together again. Learn to live with the chair in pieces for longer than you expected, and accept the challenge of a series of operations when you thought you would only have to carry out one.

Next there is the question of when to clean the

wood, or strip off the chair for refinishing – before or after you reassemble it. The order in which you tackle these jobs is not critical, but you may find it more convenient to strip the old finish off each member on its own, rather than work on the reassembled chair when some parts will be difficult to get at.

But let us presume that you can go ahead with the reassembly immediately and enjoy the satisfaction of a completed job.

GLUE

Two main types of glue are available to the furniture restorer – Scotch glue, the traditional woodworking adhesive, and white resin PVA glue.

Scotch glue is becoming increasingly difficult to find. Old-established ironmongers generally keep a stock, and it is worth locating a supplier. Buy half a kilogram, and it should last you for years.

PVA glue comes in plastic bottles and is available through all d-i-y shops. Buy a small bottle. It has a convenient spout and you will waste less through drying out.

Some conscientioius restorers would never dream of using anything but Scotch glue. Their main concern is future restorers, who will have a far easier time dismantling the work if Scotch glue has been used. This can also be a great advantage to the beginner. If the assembly turns out to be wrong – and some of your efforts almost certainly will – you can dismantle the chair and start again.

The problem with Scotch glue is that it sets by cooling. It is applied hot and you must have the joint assembled quickly – within seconds rather than minutes – so that the joint is held firm and in the right place as the glue begins to cool. By the time the glue has cooled to room temperature, it has set, and in a few days it will be rock-hard. Working in a warm workshop, and closing all doors and windows to eliminate draughts, will help to slow down the setting rate.

PVA glue sets far more slowly. It needs no preparation and you apply it straight from the container. It begins to bite within a couple of hours and sets hard within about twelve. This gives you time to go about your assembly with greater care and far less risk of going wrong

through hurrying. On the other hand, since the glue is water-resistant, you will face a long and tedious process of apply damp heat to soften it once it has set hard.

Have both sorts available. PVA resin glue has its place, for example where you are letting in new wood and no future restorer is ever likely to want to take it out again. Scotch glue, on the other hand, although it needs careful preparation, is more interesting to use. If you can learn to work quickly enough to get the assembly right, it is certainly safer for the amateur.

Preparing Scotch glue

To prepare Scotch glue you will need a double heating system. Purpose-made glue-pots are available. They consist of an outer container in which you boil water and an inner container in which the glue heats and softens. Although professionals always use them, they get messy, and cleaning them can be unpleasant.

A perfectly adequate alternative for amateurs is a small saucepan in which to boil water with a jam jar or tin can inside to hold the glue. Put a 13mm layer of glue pearls in the bottom of the jar and add water to cover the pearls by another 13mm. Use plenty of water in the outer container or saucepan, and heat it slowly. Never put the cold jam jar into hot water, or add cold water round the hot jam jar, or it will crack.

Your ironmonger may stock a special glue-brush, or you can cut down an old 13mm paint brush providing you clean it well.

The glue is ready for use when it runs easily off the brush. If it is too thick, slowly add boiling water. If it is too thin, add more glue pearls. When your glue-pot becomes messy, throw away the jam jar and start again. Scotch glue sets faster with repeated re-heating, so it is wise to work with small quantities and discard it from time to time.

When the glue is hot and runny, bring the workpiece and glue-pot close together. A gas ring in your workshop is ideal, so that you can keep the glue hot on the ring as you work. Otherwise, take the entire glue-pot, double boiler or saucepan to the work. The hot water will help to keep the glue warm.

Wherever possible, hold the work over the pot for glueing, so that the excess runs back into the pot, not over the floor or the work itself. If you are glueing a length of wood, run the wood along the top of the pot, holding the glue-brush steady. If you are glueing a joint, just brush a thin layer over it. Do not worry about glueing inside mortices. The glue will find its way under pressure to all the parts that need it, and the excess will ooze out of the joint.

Cramps

All major woodworking operations involve cramping up the work at some stage, therefore a good set of cramps is essential.

To cramp up a chair you will need two sash-cramps. They are available in various lengths; however, one pair of 90cm cramps is enough for most jobs.

It is possible to save money by buying only the sash-cramp heads. You can then cut a piece of wood for each pair, the right width and thickness to fit through the heads. The head with the tightening handle fits on one end, and you can drill holes at 50mm intervals along the length of the wood to accommodate the peg on the moveable head.

If you subsequently encounter a job for which your cramps are too short, you can cut more wood to make a pair to the required length.

You will also need several softwood pads to protect the workpiece from the metal faces of the cramps. Never work without this protection: the metal will press ugly marks into the hardest of woods. Soft pads cut from cork tiles, and actually glued to the faces of the wooden pads, help to put the kindest possible surface in contact with the workpiece.

Eventually you will also need at least one pair of G-cramps. 10cm cramps are adequate for most tasks. But if you are planning to restore several pieces, buy cramps as the need arises. You will never find that you own too many. Remember to use softwood or cork pads as well. Alternatively you can make up a tourniquet, or Spanish windlass. This consists of a loop of rope, and a stick to twist through the loop to draw it tight [2.4]. Use softwood pads, since rope can mark wood as badly as metal. You may find that a length of upholsterers' webbing, which gives even pressure over a wider area, is more successful than rope.

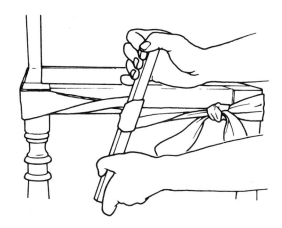

2.4a A tourniquet or Spanish windlass makes a reasonable substitute for orthodox cramps.

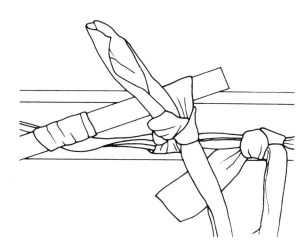

b Tie down the end of the rod to prevent the twist unwinding.

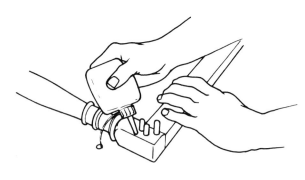

2.5 Brush or spread glue on the joint.

Tightening the tourniquet can produce an adequate cramping operation. But it is at best a makeshift device. Sash-cramps give controlled pressure at each of the joints. The difference is remarkable, so if you are at all serious, buy some.

REASSEMBLING A CHAIR

First try a 'dry run' to ensure that all the joints go together. They should be a close fit. If they are too tight, rub down the tenons or the dowels with glasspaper.

Set up the cramps, with the pads, to fit the workpiece. You will not have time to adjust the cramp heads once the glue is on the wood. Lay the cramps handily to the sides of the work. If you can, warm the joints slightly by putting the wood in an oven. It will slow down the cooling of the glue and give you more time to work.

With everything ready – and if possible a mate handy to hold the parts in place while you work – start glueing up the joints. Brush on the glue and slot the joints home in turn [2.5]. Put on the cramps and tighten them up: not too tight; the cramps are designed to hold the joints steady while the glue dries, not to compress them into a good fit. If excessive pressure is used, the joints will come under a reverse pressure once you have removed the cramps and will soon work loose.

Once you have the cramps on, check them carefully. They should be in identical positions on each side of the workpiece. Check the levels. If they are pulling in non-parallel directions, the chair will tend to twist, and set out of true. Make sure that the pressure from the cramps is directly against the joint itself, or again the work will be pulled out of true [2.6].

When all the cramps are correctly positioned, wipe away the excess glue with a cloth soaked in hot water and wrung out. Leave the job untouched for twenty-four hours, then you can take off the cramps. The chair should have a satisfying sturdy feel about it. Now, all that remains is to replace the corner blocks and the pegs.

The blocks rarely fit exactly and menacing gaps often appear between the blocks and chair rails. This is not vitally important. The joints themselves should be accurate enough to maintain the 'set' of the chair, and the blocks are there merely to help to brace the joints. Fit the blocks dry first, then remove them, glue them where they make contact, and screw them home, just enough to hold and not enough to put the joints under stress.

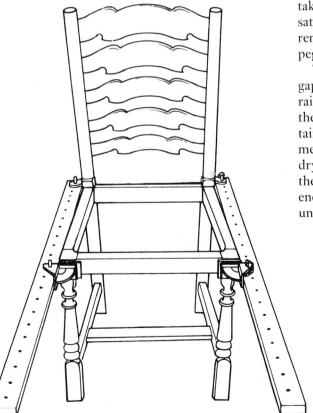

2.6   Cramp up the joints to a snug but not over-tight fit.

2.7 Trim the end of the peg or dowel and cut a shallow channel for the glue to escape.

To fit the pegs, buy a length of dowel corresponding to the diameter of the holes. Measure the depth of each hole and cut the dowel at least 13mm over length. Trim the end with a chisel so that the peg will slot home without chipping, and either trim a tiny sliver of wood off one side or cut a shallow groove to allow the excess glue to escape. Dip the end of the peg in the heated Scotch glue or squeeze out a ring of PVA round the end. Push the peg into the hole and tap it home with a mallet. Leave to dry before trimming.

Some pegs are trimmed flush with the surface of the surrounding wood, especially in modern furniture. Other pegs, most notably in old oak furniture, are designed to stand slightly proud and form a small wooden knob or dome. Your notebook sketches should tell you how your chair was originally made. If the pegs are to be left proud, trim them carefully with a sharp chisel.

Modern dowelling is generally made from ramin, a wood that works easily. If you are restoring a high-quality antique, however, you should use the same wood that the maker used. It will probably be the same as that of the chair itself – for example oak in an oak chair. This means that you will have to cut your own pegs, just as the original maker did.

Access to a lathe on which you can turn pegs would be ideal. Most people will have to use simpler methods. Plane down a piece of wood to the same thickness as the diameter of the hole. Then saw and plane a length from it to form a square peg. Plane off the corners to give an eight-sided section, then run it through your hand while you hold a piece of medium-grade glasspaper in your palm. You should produce a length of dowel, round in section and accurate enough to form a good strong peg. Cut it to length, cut a groove for the glue to escape and fit and trim the peg as before [**2.7**].

A more accurate way of producing a peg involves a little elementary metalwork. You will need a piece of mild steel about 6mm thick. A piece from an old bedstead is about right, or you may be able to buy a length at a local steelyard. About 200mm is long enough to hold in a vice. Drill a hole through it, using a high-speed metal bit of exactly the same gauge as the hole in the mortice. You can drill other holes for other sizes of pegs or dowels you want to make.

Now chisel out a rough peg from hardwood, a fraction larger than the size you finally want. Using a mallet, knock the peg through the drilled hole. The metal will neatly strip off the outside wood, leaving you with a peg of exactly the required size. In fact it will be slightly over-size, as the steel will have compressed it slightly as you forced it through the hole. It will then give a good tight fit when it is compressed once more on being slotted into the joint.

If you do not have a vice and sturdy bench to hold the steel while you manufacture your pegs, support the steel on a pair of slightly separated blocks or bricks on a solid floor.

There is one further complication. Many pegs are either purely decorative or are designed merely to prevent a joint working loose. Some, however, especially in early hand-made chairs, are an integral part of the joint. The joint is drilled so that the holes in the tenon and surrounding wood do not exactly correspond but are offset by about 2mm. As the peg is hammered home it draws the holes into line, forming a joint as tight as a cramped one.

During the dry run for reassembling the chair, look into the peg holes and see if the hole in the tenon is offset. If it is, you will have to follow a

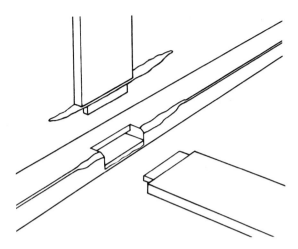

2.8 Serious damage such as this, where a back upright has split, will require extensive renovation.

Each problem makes its own demands. However, the principles behind letting in new wood are the same for all cases, and it is possible to demonstrate them in a few typical examples. You will find as you work through one operation that the steps apply to a wide range of jobs.

First you will have to identify the wood from which the furniture is constructed – not always easy under a covering of stain, polish, and layers of dirt. Descriptions in a book are of limited use. A more reliable way is to buy a few samples from a hardwood dealer and handle them until you can recognise the species wherever you find it.

Use paint stripper to remove the polish from the damaged part to reveal the grain without doing any harm. Then find a sample of the wood with the nearest possible grain pattern. Make sure, of course, that the grain runs the same way. The new piece must be bigger in length, width and thickness than the affected part that you intend to remove.

A problem afflicting badly dilapidated chairs provides a typical example of the need to let in new wood. The fault occurs where the stresses have not only loosened the joint in the way already dealt with, but have broken wood away from the back around the mortice [2.8].

Where two tenons enter the upright from the two sides, only a narrow strut of wood is left at the inner corner. So long as the joint is securely glued, the arrangement is perfectly sound, since each part of the joint derives strength from its adhesion to the other parts. But once the joint begins to work loose, individual parts have to take stress on their own. The narrow section between the two mortices is vulnerable, and rapidly deteriorates. The only solution is to take out all the damaged and weakened wood and let in a new piece.

Do not be afraid to take out plenty of wood. The greater the surface area connecting the new wood to the old, the stronger the joint will be. On the other hand there is no point in making a new piece too big: the repair may become so obvious that you would be better advised to make an entirely new member. You must also consider the value of the piece as an antique. The fewer repairs, the more valuable it will be. Getting the right balance between these conflicting interests is something you can only develop with practice.

slightly different sequence. Measure and cut your pegs during the dry run. During re-assembly, as soon as you have the joints glued and pushed home, apply glue to the pegs and tap them in. If the chair is accurately made, it should not be necessary to use cramps at all, though they will help to hold the chair steady while the glue dries.

If you have carried out the steps so far described you will have learned a great deal about furniture restoration – dismantling, cleaning up, glueing and cramping. However complicated these processes become on more difficult pieces, the basic techniques remain the same.

LETTING IN NEW WOOD

By replacing parts of the old wood with new, what looks like a terminal case can be brought back to perfectly sound condition. The procedure is far easier than it looks, and, if done well, only close examination will reveal that grafting has taken place.

New wood is needed to correct a variety of faults. A serious attack of woodworm, simply rot, or a fracture in which dirt, splintered fragments or missing wood make straightforward re-glueing impossible.

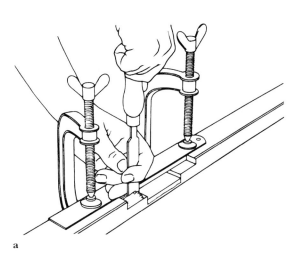

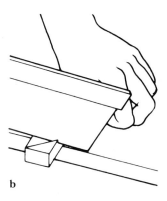

b

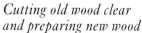

a

2.9a   Letting in new wood, a similar process for many types of repair, involves first cutting away old wood using a mortice chisel and working to a straight line. Cramp a steel ruler to the workpiece and tidy up the recess with a paring chisel.

b   Prepare the new wood, with the face and edge planed perfectly flat, and cut it slightly overlength, with the ends angled to form 'dovetails'.

Cutting old wood clear and preparing new wood

To clear away the damaged wood, first scribe lines along the chair's rear post using a straight edge. These form base lines, one for each new mortice to be cut. The best place to scribe the base line is exactly at the side of the original mortice, away from the damaged wood. The old joint provides the best guide and the new will be in precisely the same place.

Now chisel out the wood. The correct tool to use is a mortice chisel (also known as a sash-mortice chisel). This has a strong blade of constant width, designed to cut across the grain. Hold it exactly against the side of the guide line, and hit it sharply with a mallet. It will cut a wedge into the wood. Move it along, in the direction of its face, still using the scribed line as a guide. Make another cut, then a third, and so on. Each cut should break away a narrow wedge of wood. If not, simply slide the chisel along under the chippings to free them.

Go to either end of the damaged area, working from both sides if they are accessible. Chisel to the depth required as accurately as you can.

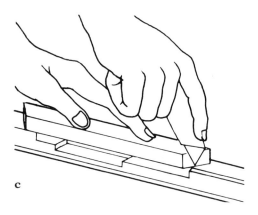

c

c   Lay the new wood in place over the workpiece and mark the cutting angle at the ends.

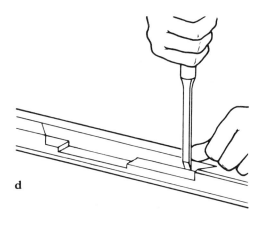

d

d   Cut out the angled recess.

Working with the mortice chisel will not produce perfectly flat sides to the recess. So cramp a straight edge on to the workpiece, exactly on the position of the scribed line; a steel rule is ideal and will bend to fit a curved surface. Then use an ordinary paring chisel to clean away the wood up to the line. You will have to rely on your eye to ensure that the chisel is exactly upright [**2.9a**].

At the ends of the joint, it is advisable to let in a 'dovetail'. The idea is to cut the ends of the joint at an angle, so that the load it will carry in use falls against the wood itself, and does not rely on the strength of the glue alone. Examine the workpiece and see which way the load falls. In the case of a chair it will be in the front-to-back direction, so you should form the 'dovetail' on the side. First, however, prepare the new wood.

Plane an accurate face side and face edge on to your selected piece. It should be long enough to fill the new recess and thick enough to leave plenty over. Next, saw the piece to length, cutting the ends to form the dovetail. An angle of about 60 degrees will give a sturdy joint. Mark one end and saw it through. Hold the wood over the recess to give a cut slightly longer than the recess itself and mark and saw the other end. Clean off the 'feathers' – the tiny splinters left by the saw.

Now return to the chair back. Hold the new piece as accurately as possible in place and mark the angles [**2.9c**]. Chisel out the waste [**2.9d**]; care and perseverance will produce a clean cut. The new piece should fit precisely, but remain proud by a generous amount. This will be removed later.

If it does not fall into place comfortably, pare away the excess. Small gaps can be filled in later with some form of 'stopping'. If there are large gaps, reject the piece and make a new one. Do not try to make the new piece fit the existing recess. Cut it slightly longer, then re-work the angled ends of the recess to match the new piece.

Finishing the repair

When you are satisfied with the fit, glue the new wood in place. Permanent PVA glue is acceptable as this is not a part of the piece that will ever need to be dismantled and reassembled. If the repair ever proved faulty, a future restorer would cut away wood by the same process.

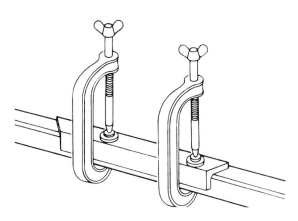

2.10a Glue the new wood in place, cramping it up firmly with protective pads.

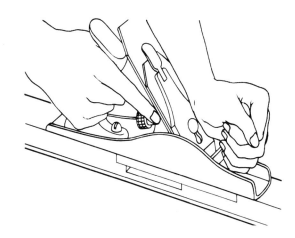

b Plane off the excess wood level with the workpiece surface, on both the face and the edge.

Apply glue sparingly to the recess and slot home the new wood. Protecting the piece with offcuts of soft wood, cramp it in place from two directions with even pressure. Leave the glue to harden thoroughly overnight.

Once the glue has set, secure the workpiece in a vice and plane off the excess wood. If other parts of the chair prevent you reaching the new wood with a plane, pare it down with a chisel. Theoretically you should stop when you have planed the new piece flush with the existing wood, but in practice it is worth taking a thin shaving off the old wood to ensure a perfectly uniform surface [**2.10**].

In many repairs involving letting in new wood you can now go on to re-finish the piece.

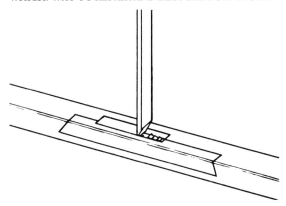

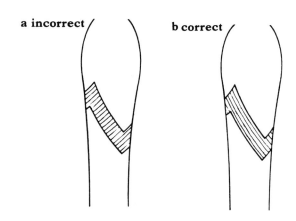

2.11 Mark the line of the new mortice with a mortice gauge and cut the new joint with a mortice chisel.

2.12 Examine the grain to ensure that shoulder of a splice does not include a 'short' grain.

If stripping off the old finish, spread stripper liberally over the existing wood and the new wood together. The stripper and any old polish and dirt will help merge the two surfaces. Wash the area with methylated spirits. (See page 48 for details of stripping procedures.)

If you are repairing broken chair joints, re-cut the mortices using a mortice chisel the same width as the tenon [2.11]. If you originally used the edge of the old mortice as your base line, then the edge of the new wood will provide the perfect line from which to work. Alternatively, providing the piece has a flat face and edge, you can use a mortice gauge. Set the points the same width apart as the thickness of the tenon and slide the moving block along to the appropriate measurement from the face and edge of the wood, then turn the screw firmly to hold the measurement.

Of course, if working on a curved piece of wood you cannot use its face as a guide. The simplest method then is to hold the tenon in place, slide a steel rule up against it, remove the tenon and scribe a line against the steel rule.

Sharpen the mortice chisel, cut the new mortice in the new wood using the wedge-chipping technique already described, and clean up the edges. Try the rail in place. The tenon should be a tight fit in the mortice.

Turn the chair-post over and cut the second mortice. But take care: completing the second mortice leaves an extremely thin section of wood between the two joints. Avoid breaking this by keeping your chisel razor sharp and finish the cutting process by hand alone, without a mallet.

With any necessary re-cutting of the mortices complete, the chair should be ready for reassembly as already described.

OTHER CHAIR REPAIRS

Broken legs

Broken chair legs often appear to be so irreparable that the owner may be tempted to discard the chair altogether. In fact, if the leg has suffered a clean fracture, it may be possible to glue and cramp it together leaving hardly any sign of a break.

Frequently, you will have to cut away the splinters and let in a splice of new wood. The repair will involve dismantling the chair to use one leg as a pattern for the length and shape of the other. The splice should be cut on the slant, and the ends must incorporate a shoulder, or the faces of the joint will slide across each other as weight is applied to the chair.

These shoulders can themselves be vulnerable if the new wood is cut with the grain in the wrong direction. A weak shoulder, with a short grain, is shown in figure [2.12a]. A properly cut splice is illustrated in figure [2.12b]. Plane the wood for the splice first. It must be large enough to incorporate the shoulder, to cover the damaged wood and to leave some spare for removing later. Scribe the two faces to be glued and with a try-square mark in the shoulders.

Secure the wood in a vice and saw along the two faces as far as the shoulders. Then turn the piece and saw through to make the shoulders.

With a marking knife, transfer the outline of the splice to the broken chair leg. If the leg is in two parts, tape the broken pieces to the good leg to secure them in their correct respective positions. Pack slivers of wood between the legs to accommodate any tapering. Saw along the lines, to remove the damaged wood, cutting in the shoulders exactly as on the splice itself.

The three parts should now fit together as in [2.12a]. Without doubt, this kind of freehand cutting will lead to fitting problems. Pare down all the high spots until the fit is perfect, taking care not to slice the shoulders off with over-enthusiastic use of the chisel.

Glueing the pieces together will test your ingenuity with cramps; in theory, pressure from the ends should be enough to hold the joints closed while the glue dries, but in practice you will need to rig up a system that also holds the surfaces together. On a simple chair leg, try this with a sash-cramp along the length, and two G-cramps at the joint. Check the set of the leg from every angle, to make sure that you are not building a twist into it.

When the glue has dried, remove excess wood with a plane on the flat surfaces, and a spokeshave on the curves. Stain and polish the finished leg, then reassemble the chair.

An alternative preferred by some restorers is to let metal into the leg to hold the joints together. Lengths of 6mm round steel section, with the ends filed to remove any burr, are ideal. Cut them long enough to pass through the splice and about 40mm into each part of the leg. With this method there is no need to cut shoulders, and sawing the mating faces also becomes easier. You cannot, of course, use steel where you need to cut joints across the mating faces.

When cutting the splice, mark and saw its faces so that they are not precisely parallel but form a slight wedge shape.

Now tape the broken leg to the good one and scribe lines on to it to match the splice. Saw the leg cleanly to make way for the splice. With the leg parts held firmly in position, put a spot of glue on one face and slide the splice between the two parts until the wedge makes a firm contact on both faces.

The glue makes a temporary fix between the splice and one part of the leg. When it is dry

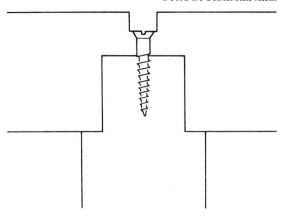

2.13 A screw, covered by a plug, may be used to draw a joint together and help ensure a firm hold.

remove the unglued part and drill holes through the splice and the part to which it is glued. Make these deep enough to take the reinforcing rods but do not insert them yet.

First glue the other part of the leg to the splice, permanently. Continue to use the sound matching leg as a guide to length. Cramp the parts together.

When the splice and one part of the leg are firmly glued, hold the assembly in a vice and break away the part that was temporarily joined. A tap with a mallet and softwood pad should do it. The holes through the splice will now be revealed and you can drill through them into the permanently fixed part of the leg. Measure the depth of hole with a probe to make sure that they will take the rods. Finally, insert the rods and glue the other part permanently, cramping along the length and width. Plane, shave and sand off excess wood, and stain and polish the repair.

An adaptation of this method, where no new splice is needed, is to reinforce a cracked or broken chair member with a bracing screw. If the crack is old you may have to break it completely to clear out the accumulated grime. If new, you may be able to prise it open to work glue into it. It may be possible to cramp up the joint without glue, drill pilot holes and a recess to take a plug, then use the screw alone to draw the joint tight after inserting glue. Otherwise, glue and cramp it, and, when the glue has dried, drill the pilot hole to take the bracing screw [2.13].

A pilot hole should be the depth of the screw and wide enough to allow the thread to bite without splitting the wood. Before inserting the screw, drill out a small recess to take a plug, slightly wider than the screw head.

Carve a small plug to fit the recess, with the grain matching as far as possible the character of the surrounding wood. Do not cut the plug with the end grain showing.

As you glue and cramp the joint, screw home the bracing screw, glue in the plug, and, when the glue has set, plane it down to match the surface. Stain and polish it and the repair will be barely visible.

With a woodworking lathe you can turn your own pegs or dowels from hardwood and use these in place of steel rods. This is a more elegant solution and adds some strength to the joint by using material which, unlike steel, bonds with the glue. Do not use ready-made dowel; it is cut from softwood, or ramin, which is not strong enough to take stresses across its grain, and is likely to snap. Turn the pegs fractionally oversize and cut a glue-escape channel in them. Pegs can be used to mend breakages at almost any point in a chair.

Victorian chairs, for example [2.14] often give way near the point where a curved top rail joins a curved back upright. Since the top rail is cut from a single piece of wood, the grain lies along the length on the main part, but runs across the wood where it curves. This 'short grain' at the joints is under considerable stress and often breaks.

The solution is to peg in a new wood. If only one side of the chair is broken, release the opposite joint to complete the dismantling. If this is well fixed, you may have to saw through it – thereby losing a fraction of the wood – rather than wrench the joint and risk bruising the wood.

Cut the useless wood away from the damaged area to make room for the splicing piece. Lay the chair out to a pattern and cut the new piece to fit between the end of the rail and the upright post. Then proceed as on the spliced leg. Glue the splice to the rail with temporary dabs of glue and drill it to take a hardwood or steel peg. Release it, and glue the splice to the top of the upright. Let pegs into these two parts together. Before finally glueing the joint, attend to the other end of the rail. If you have had to cut any pegs in dismantling, scrape out the remaining wood to leave the original holes clear and clean. Re-making the joint will then be easy.

If damaged wood makes it impossible to use the original holes, drill new ones. To start them in the same place on corresponding faces, first make a small indentation at a suitable point on the face with a hammer and punch. Rest a small ball-bearing in the indentation, fit the other piece as closely as possible, and tap it lightly with a mallet and softwood pad. The ball-bearing leaves a matching indentation. The real difficulty lies in drilling holes in the right direction. If the faces are square enough you can put the pieces in a vice and drill into them exactly perpendicularly.

After a satisfactory 'dry' assembly, glue the joints home.

Saddles

Because chairs are not made up of rectangular members, cramping them can be extremely difficult, and if not done properly can lead to the finished article being warped.

Cramps must not be put on at the best available angle and tightened up regardless. Instead, the curved lines of the chair should be converted into straight lines, to accommodate the stresses of the cramping operation, by making up 'saddles'. These are pieces of softwood cut to fit the curves of a chair or any other piece of furniture. The outer side to which the cramps are applied remains straight and square, and the tightening action of the cramp is distributed evenly and in the right direction over the curved area.

Cutting saddles might seem a tedious business because a new one must be made for each operation. Fortunately, since the introduction of the power jig-saw, the task has become simpler. Trace the outline of the chair-back on to a piece of cardboard, transfer the outline by means of pin holes on to the wood and cut round the curve with a power saw. A few strokes with a spokeshave will remove any high spots and give the saddle a perfect fit.

With wood-carving tools you can cut a groove in the saddle to match precisely the curved section of the chair-back [2.15].

Another type consists of a piece of wood, recessed to accommodate the chair piece, and a length of leather nailed into position to fit to the curved shape of the back [2.16].

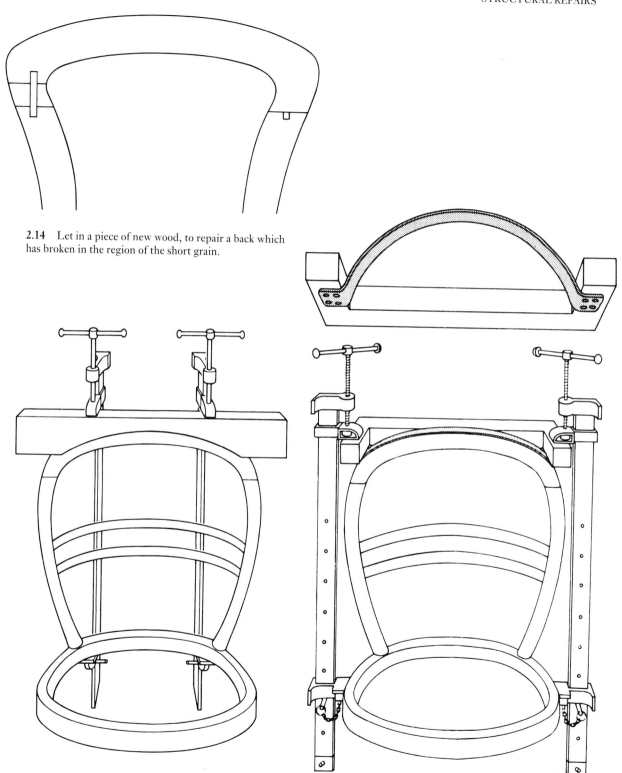

2.14 Let in a piece of new wood, to repair a back which has broken in the region of the short grain.

2.15 A simple saddle, cut and grooved, will give even pressure when cramping curved articles.

2.16 Alternatively a wood-and-leather apparatus can be rigged up to accommodate complex curves.

29

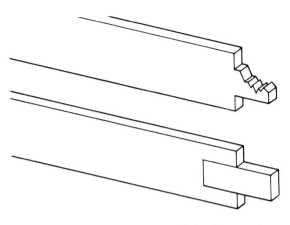

2.17 A remade tenon will produce a joint almost as strong as the original.

Broken joints

If a chair has been subjected to excessive stress, the housing of the joints may stay firm, but the inner part crack and break off [**2.17**]. It is possible to repair this by letting new wood into the rail, effectively converting the joint into a double-mortice. First saw and chisel away the broken part of the tenon. Measure the original mortice and mark it on the surface from which the tenon was cut away. Chisel out this member to a suitable depth and prepare a new piece of wood to fit the recess. Glued in place, the new wood should look exactly as the original tenon. Beech, which is not difficult to work, but has the strength and tightness of grain to carry the load of such a joint, is an ideal wood to use.

TABLE REPAIRS

Many of the problems with tables are similar to those with chairs. The operations follow the same sequence. First assess the job. Dismantle the furniture if necessary. Let in new wood to replace the damaged part or make a new member entirely if the damage is extensive. If the surface is damaged it will be a matter of reglueing veneer, cutting in new veneer, or simply cleaning and repolishing.

However, there are other difficulties, many of them the result of shrinkage, which are peculiar to tables. A table is basically a frame, with a flat board fitted to the top. Most antique tables were perfectly satisfactory in the places for which they were designed. Even if the rooms were well heated by fires, the draught of the fire brought plenty of moist air in from outside. Low humidity – the real cause of shrinkage – was not a significant problem. The introduction of central heating changed the balance drastically. Now, throughout the winter months, a table may stand in an atmosphere which is much drier than the outdoor air. The air in the room remains virtually static, unlike the situation in rooms with open hearths and chimneys. Double glazing can add to the problem by further eliminating draughts.

The result is that the wood steadily dries out and over a long period, shrinks. Serious trouble arises because wood only shrinks in one direction, across the grain. In other words, a plank becomes narrower, but not appreciably shorter.

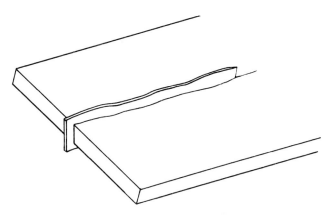

2.18 Let in a fillet of wood to repair a table which has cracked through shrinkage.

The construction of antique furniture took no account of this, and cabinet-makers happily joined together parts with the grain running in opposing directions. When bonded pieces of wood shrink at different rates, the stresses are more than any glue can stand, and it gives way. Veneers lift from their ground, parts separate from each other, or, where parts are well screwed in place, the wood itself splits.

Repairing splits
There are two methods of repairing splits: closing them up, or letting in new wood. The method adopted determines whether you dismantle a table or deal with the repair *in situ*. It is possible to let in new wood with the table-top in place, but to close the split you will have to separate the top from the frame. Generally, whatever the operation, working on fully dismantled furniture gives better results.

Often, when the table-top is a single piece, it splits only part of the way across the surface: because as the stress is released, there is no need for it to split further. In closing up such a gap you will only revive the original stresses. In such cases the kind of repair illustrated in [2.18] is advised.

First saw down the length of the crack. It is impossible to make a piece of wood to fit accurately the narrow triangular shape this kind of split makes. The thickness of a saw cut is often enough to make the sides of the fault parallel. Next, insert a small fillet of wood. Your success with this kind of repair depends on how closely you can match the thickness of the inserted wood to the thickness of the saw blade. A better repair is made by using a narrow-backed saw such as a coping saw, or better still a fretsaw. Make the cut follow the curve in the split, which will itself follow the grain, and thus remove the minimum amount of wood. Now cut a slice of wood, such as a thick veneer, slightly oversize. Glue the mating faces, insert it in to the cut and cramp up the table-top from both sides. When the glue has set, plane down the insert and finally scrape it dead level before polishing.

If the crack is too wide to clean out with a single saw cut, first make a saw cut at the narrow end, where the saw is in contact with both faces. Insert the fillet glued on one side only. When the glue has set, make a second cut, working carefully along the side of the first fillet. Slide a second fillet, glued on both sides, down beside the first.

Cracks are liable to develop on a table of the kind illustrated in [2.19a]. The top is in two halves which are joined together; the screws fixing it to the oval frame are concealed under round-headed knobs. Many of these elegant tables were designed to tilt vertically, to form a decorative screen. Central heating can shrink the top and leave a crack of 2mm or more between the two halves.

To repair, carefully ease out the plugs and remove the screws holding the top to the frame. Then screw them home again with the gap closed up. If the boards are to be glued together, you may have to cut new bars for your sash cramps especially for this operation. Alternatively, lay the two parts of the table-top on an absolutely flat surface, pass a rope, or better still a length of leather, round them and cramp up the end. If the rope or leather is nailed to two blocks, as in the arrangement illustrated in [2.19c], you can draw the blocks together with G-cramps.

Otherwise the wedging system [2.19d] may work. Again you need a firm base, such as a long plank of wood or two laid parallel. Screw a block of wood at one end to form a fixed post against which the compression can act. Screw down a second block at the other end, about 150mm further away than the width of the piece being glued. Cut a third block in half diagonally to form two triangular pieces. They will serve as wedges. Set them up so that the inclined faces work against each other, and tap them from opposite ends with a mallet. The 'rectangle' you have formed will gradually increase in width, forcing the two parts of the workpiece together.

If the crack has not produced warping, and can be pulled together without too much pressure, it may well be possible to repair the damage by simply holding the gap closed. Glue alone will not withstand the pressure, but the system illustrated in [2.20] usually works. The 'butterflies', forming a kind of double-dovetail, fit on the underside of the work. Cut them with the grain running from end to end. Use well-seasoned hardwood, so later shrinking across the grain will not loosen them.

Cut the butterflies first. Their size depends on the size and weight of the table-top being repaired; 50mm–75mm is generally appropriate, 20mm–25mm at the waist is about the right

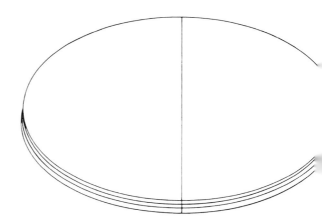

2.19a   The two halves of this type of table may drift apart through the effects of central heating.

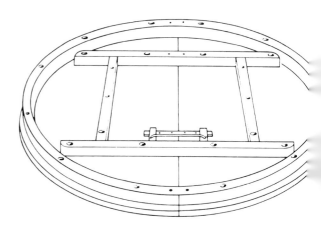

b   The top boards will have to be removed from the frame and re-fixed, with the two parts closed up.

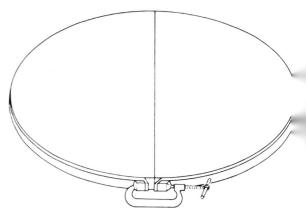

c   Cramping the repair using a strap, two blocks and a G-cramp.

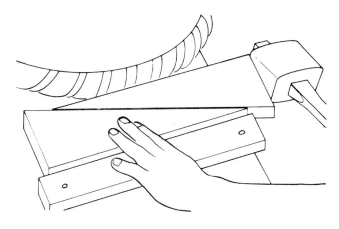

d Alternatively, rig up a wedging system. Tapping the wedges together will close the gap in the table-top.

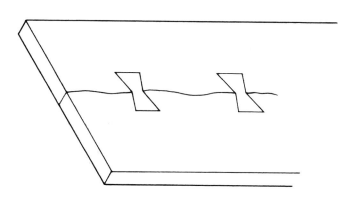

2.20 Cut and insert 'butterflies' to hold the repair after closing a crack in a relatively flexible board.

width. On most table-tops, they should be about 6mm thick when in place. Cut them over-thick. Only the bottom face needs to be planed flat. The other face will be planed off when the butterfly is in place.

Cramp the table-top to close the split, and position the butterflies. Mark each according to where it goes and in which direction it lies. Then scribe round them. Release the cramps and you can now cut the recesses to take the butterflies. The right tool to use is the mortice chisel, which will cut down into the wood of the table-top across the grain. When you have made the downward cuts, clean out the bottom of the recess with a paring chisel.

Cramp up the piece again and check that the butterflies are a close fit. Release the cramps so that you can brush glue into the split itself and on to the bed of each recess. Cramp up again, put the butterflies in place and weight them, protected with wax paper to prevent the weights sticking to the work. When the glue has dried, plane the butterflies flush with the surface and protect them with a coat of polish.

When you have repaired a table-top by closing the split, you will find that the screw holes in the frame no longer line up exactly with the positions of the screws in the top, but are too close to the original holes to drill firm new ones. The solution is to turn the table-top right round. The old holes are unlikely to line up again and you can drill new ones.

Hinges

Drop-leaf tables, such as gate-leg tables, can suffer too from shrinkage and warping. There may be no serious damage from the shrinkage itself, but the narrowing of the centre board of the table means that the outer leaves do not drop clear of the frame and the hinge can be strained to breaking point. Or the centre leaf of the table may be in two pieces and they pull apart. Still more problems arise when the gate-leg is not opened fully, and weight on the outer, unsupported, section of the drop leaf leads to splitting.

The table probably needs dismantling and reassembling in a way that eliminates the cause of the trouble.

If the centre section has split, you may be able to cramp it up and glue it, preferably with butterflies. This may also work when the boards of a drop leaf have come apart. However, if you deal with the centre section in this way, you will have to make sure that there is still room for the drop leaves to fall clear of the frame. If not, the solution may be to let in a separate piece down the centre gap.

If the hinges have pulled loose, you will have to re-fit them. It will almost certainly be impossible to fix the screws near their former holes, and you will have to move the hinge to a new position. Before you do so, clean out the old hinge recesses and let in a small fillet of new wood of the same type and character as the table.

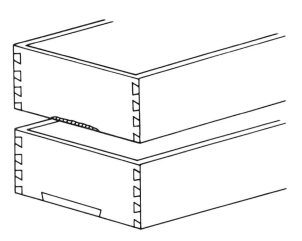

2.21 It may be necessary to let in new wood to repair the running part of a drawer which has become worn down.

CARCASS REPAIRS

'Carcass' is the trade name for the type of furniture which is basically a box. Most furniture is a frame, such as a chair, or a box, or a combination of both. Boxes suffer, especially when they shrink, because the large boards from which they are formed are interlinked, and stresses are transmitted throughout the structure. By the time an amateur restorer has repaired chairs and tables, he or she should have no difficulty in working on carcasses, even though they are generally bigger and less accessible.

Drawers

Most carcasses incorporate drawers. In time the wooden runners on which they slide are worn down, even to the point where they do not support the drawer at all.

Sometimes the drawer has simply warped, probably as the result of drying out due to central heating, and no longer runs freely. The answer is to plane wood off the part of the drawer which is sticking. Take care not to remove too much wood, and rub a block of beeswax on the bare wood to help it run smoothly.

Take out any drawer and examine its construction. If it has the grooves in the drawer sides you will see whether the upper edge has worn, and

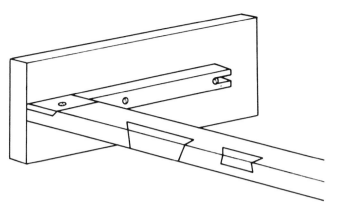

2.22 If the runner itself is worn, it will need to be replaced. Slot-screw it at the rear, to accommodate later shrinkage. If the wear extends to the front rail, cut away the worn part and let in new wood.

whether the corresponding upper edge of the runner, fixed to the inside of the carcass, has worn too. To cure the trouble, recut the groove in the side of the drawer. Do this with a small circular saw, on which you can set the depth, with a batten cramped firmly to the piece at the right distance to hold the saw blade on the correct line. Chisel out the surplus wood afterwards to give a smooth running surface. You will then have to remake the runner on the inside of the carcass. The best plan is to prise out the original, and either replace it entirely with a wider one, or set it higher in the drawer side and turn it upside down to expose a fresh edge. If possible, follow the original method of fixing. Rub both parts with beeswax to cut down wear from friction in the future.

Other types of drawers sit on runners. Often there is a rail across the front of the carcass, and maybe a dustboard to separate the drawer compartments. If the side of the drawer shows wear on its lower edge, as in [**2.21**], repair it by cutting away the wood to square it up and glueing another piece in its place. It will probably be necessary to cut and plane it to the exact size before fitting it, as the lip of the drawer will prevent working with a plane when the new wood is in place. On the runner you will probably find a deep indentation along its entire length. Ideally, the new runner should be glued in position at the

front and slot-screwed at the back to allow for expansion and contraction in the side-boards [**2.22**].

If the indentation extends as far forwards as the rail across the front, you will have to dismantle the carcass, cut away the worn wood to give you a square bed, and let in a new piece [**2.22**].

On most types of drawer, the rail and the bottom board should carry a couple of wooden stops. If they are missing, serious problems can follow. The drawer itself may run right in, and slam against the back of the cabinet. Or, especially on furniture of the early eighteenth century, the lip that was used to conceal the drawer opening will have taken the full force of the drawer closing and will have broken off. The lip was commonly glued into a rebate round the front of the drawer, with a decorative veneered facing to the join. Curing the fault may involve drastic, but fortunately not complicated, treatment. It is not difficult to remove veneer.

One way is to cover the facing in damp sawdust so that the moisture seeps through to soften the glue. If in a hurry, a damp cloth and an iron will soften the glue, and you can lift the veneer. After that, remove the lip, repair it and glue the veneer back into its original position. Finally, you can polish it.

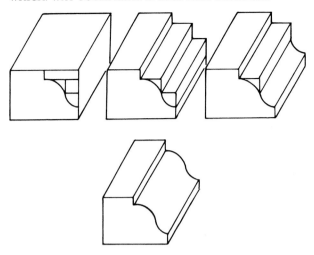

2.23a The profile of a moulding, showing the cuts necessary to produce the shape on which the final moulding can be chiselled.

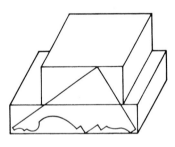

b Large mouldings can be made more cheaply from two pieces of wood.

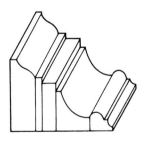

c Complicated mouldings are simply assembled from several pieces.

MOULDINGS

Do not be dismayed to find moulding broken and parts of it missing. It is common. You can remake mouldings using a power saw with a disc-type blade, either hand-held or inverted for use as a bench saw.

To reproduce a complete length, fit the wood first, by measuring and cutting the mitre at the corners. Then draw the outline of the moulding on the new wood and proceed with cuts.

If you are making several short pieces, draw the sectional outline of the moulding on to a piece of card, to use as a pattern. Draw over it a rectangle representing the width and thickness of the replacement wood. From this, as at many points as convenient, mark the distance from the face and edge, and the depth, of all the cuts. This gives the approximate outline of the moulding [**2.23a**]. The simplest way to complete the cutting is to work along the wood using a hand-held chisel with a rounded blade. This kind of chisel is sold as a wood-carving tool.

Larger and more complicated mouldings can be produced from several pieces of wood used together. [**2.23b**] shows two pieces glued to produce a large but simple profile. [**2.23c**] is a more complicated profile assembled from several separate pieces.

REPAIRS TO SURFACES

Often, a well-made article of furniture will remain structurally sound, but will need repairs to its surface which go beyond stripping and repolishing.

Leather surfaces

The leather surface of a desk or table-top is less robust than the wood which surrounds it, and a new leather or 'skiver' will be needed periodically.

Making up the new skiver, with its border of gilt tooling, is a job for the professional. Give the leather worker the dimensions of the recess in your desk top. If it is not a simple rectangle, make a template of the shape. He should be able to match the existing skiver, or, if you prefer a change, he will produce one to the right size in your specified colour.

Remove the old skiver with as little damage as possible to the surrounding woodwork. Clean away the remnants of dried glue with hot water, used sparingly, followed by a scraper. Make sure the corners and edges of the recess are absolutely clear.

You will have to repair any defects in the wood, to provide a firm base for the new skiver. Fill any splits with fillets of wood, and fill small holes with a mixture of glue and fine sawdust. Sand down the renewed surface carefully and give woodworm treatment as a precaution.

The standard technique for applying a new skiver is to glue it in place first, then cut it to fit. First try the skiver in place 'dry', to give you some idea of how the tooled border fits and how much overlap there will be all round before cutting. Prepare four or five battens – lengths of thin wood – to lie across the width of the desk. They will help to prevent excess adhesive spreading everywhere. It is also useful to have help during this operation.

Working fairly fast, spread the adhesive sparingly over the recess, and work it well into the edges and corners. Lay the wooden battens across the desk, and the new skiver across them. Lower it at one end, leaving the overlap you established when fitting it 'dry'. Ask your helper to remove the lengths of wood from under the skiver as you progress along its length, easing it gently down on to the adhesive with as little movement as possible.

With all the battens removed, the skiver should lie roughly in position. You can still make adjustments, sliding it on the adhesive. Look for the edge of the surrounding wood showing through the skiver to guide you. If the outline of the recess does not show, press all round with the back of a spoon, but not hard enough to leave a permanent creasemark.

When the skiver is correctly positioned, smooth it out from the centre, but do not press hard or you will distort the thin, wet leather. Now cut off the surrounding excess. Start near a corner, and with a scalpel make a 2cm cut in the skiver, along the line of the surrounding wood. Be extremely careful to avoid the wood, meanwhile cutting close enough to allow the skiver to fall precisely into place when pressed down. After the first incision, protect the wood and carry on cutting away towards the edge of the skiver, peeling away the strip of excess material as you go.

Press the skiver down into the edges and corners and clean off any stray adhesive as soon as possible.

Some craftsmen prefer to cut their leather tops and skivers before fitting. This can make it easier to work with, but will not give the accuracy of fit achieved by trimming in place.

Another method is to roll the skiver round a wooden rod, then, preferably with a helper, to unroll it slowly on to the pasted area, smoothing out from the centre to the sides as you go.

Repairing veneer

Broken, chipped, cracked, or lifting veneer is one of the commonest problems in furniture restoration. Look for early signs of faults in a veneered surface so that you can put them right before the damage goes too far. Trouble invariably arises from the veneer becoming detached from the 'ground' to which it is glued. Often it starts to lift at one edge, as the result of wear. Sometimes the lifting starts in the centre caused by the ground and veneer shrinking at different rates through drying out, especially in centrally heated rooms.

Trace faults by touch. First go round the edge to detect any gaps. Then go over the surface, feeling for any bumps, tapping them with a fingernail

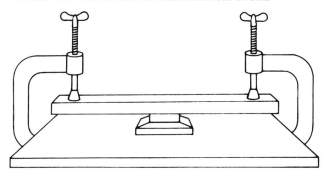

2.24   Use a shaped caul, bar and G-cramps to exert pressure on a centrally placed veneer repair.

to see if they are hollow underneath. Sometimes you can pass your hand across a surface and hear a slight hiss as you press air out of a gap. Mark with chalk the areas to be treated.

Where you still have the original veneer, repairs simply involve inserting glue between the surfaces, and pressing down the veneer until the glue sets.

However, first you must eliminate any old glue. Lift the veneer cleanly and carefully at the edge and hold it away from the ground with something like a matchstick. Use a soft brush and hot water to wash out all dirt.

In the centre of a surface, you will have to slice the veneer cleanly with a scalpel, to allow you to lift and work water under each side in turn. The veneer may be so badly buckled that you have to do this anyway to flatten it. This will not be seriously noticeable after the repair.

But to avoid making a cut at all, you may be able to drill two small holes from the underside of the ground, up into the pocket behind the lifted veneer. Gauge the depth of the drill holes with extreme care, to ensure that you do not break through the veneer and ruin the whole exercise. Use a syringe of some kind, first to run hot water through the pocket, to soften and wash out old glue, then to squirt glue into it. As you insert the glue through one hole, it should press air out of the other, until the whole pocket is filled with glue. Rub the area from the veneer side to spread the adhesive to the extreme edges of the pocket. Then apply a 'caul' until the glue sets.

A caul is a device for exerting even pressure on a veneered surface, either during its manufacture or during a repair.

At the edge of the work, a simple G-cramp with softwood pads will hold the caul well enough. For repairs some distance from the edge, a softwood pad held down by a wooden beam, with the pressure applied by cramps at both ends, will generally work. Shape the caul at the back so that the beam does not exert uneven pressure [**2.24**].

However, near the centre of large surfaces, such pressure can bend the ground, and when the cauls are taken away the surface returns to its original shape, putting the repair under strain right from the start. To avoid this problem, arrange a system of double cauls, so that your cramps exert equal pressure at the back of the repair.

If the repair to the veneer does not take well, you can complete the job with an ordinary household iron; a useful alternative method of repairing any fault where you can be sure there is no dirt behind the veneer. Use a wet cloth, and iron firmly through it. The steam heats and dampens the wood, softens the glue, and the pressure from the iron forces the surfaces together. Switch off the heat from the iron just before you start work, the iron will soften the glue, then allow the glue to cool. Simply keep the pressure on for a few minutes until the glue begins to bite.

Veneering curved surfaces presents a more difficult problem of applying uniform pressure. There are three standard solutions.

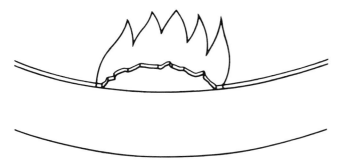

2.25 Trim round the area of an edge veneer in the shape of 'donkey's ears' to provide a clean edge for the new veneer.

The first is to bend a sheet of hardboard to fit the curved surface, and keep it in place with several cramps, exerting even pressure over the whole surface.

The second is to fill a bag with sand, lay the workpiece on it and mould the sandbag into the inverse shape of the workpiece. Apply the glue and veneer, and put the article upside down on the sandbag. Place heavy weights on the work to press it well on to the sandbag until the glue sets. Obviously, the bigger the workpiece, the less convenient this method will be.

The third method is to shape a separate piece of softwood into a curved caul to match exactly the curve of the veneered surface. On a valuable article the effort may well be worthwhile, and again the power jig-saw lessens the work. First, cut a cardboard template to match the curve exactly. Transfer the curve to the wood and cut it with the jig-saw, or with a coping saw. Make any minor adjustments with a spokeshave, and finally ensure a perfect fit by rubbing the caul and veneered surface together with a sheet of sandpaper between them. Cramping this kind of caul on to the work is straightforward.

Replacing missing veneer

Veneer tends to lift and crack particularly at the edges of surfaces, and small pieces may fall off and be lost. You will need to buy a new veneer that matches the existing surface as closely as possible.

First, prepare the existing surface to take the new wood by trimming the area of the repair. Using a scalpel, cut into the area a set of 'donkey's ears', roughly in the direction of the grain [**2.25**]. Hold the scalpel with the blade vertical. Ease up the wood you have cut away and clear all dirt and old glue off the ground.

Using masking tape, attach a piece of tracing paper large enough to cover the repair. With a soft pencil, rub in the outline of the repair, as if you were taking a brass-rubbing. Take off the paper, and tape it to the new veneer, checking that the 'ears' run in the direction of the grain. Now cut carefully round the outline with a scalpel. This time, lean the scalpel slightly away from the outline, to make the veneer fractionally oversize, and with a slight undercut. When you glue the new veneer in place, the angled edge will press firmly against the surround and produce a perfect fit. Establish the right stain and polish by trial on a waste piece of the new veneer, then stain and polish the new surface.

Inlaid banding and stringing

High-quality furniture often includes either banding or stringing. Banding is a patterned border of different woods in various colours and grains. Typically it is about 6mm–10mm wide. Stringing is a single line of wood let into the surface usually a lighter colour than the background.

Both forms of decoration are vulnerable, as the glue holding them tends to weaken with age. Then the strip begins to hang out and gets broken off.

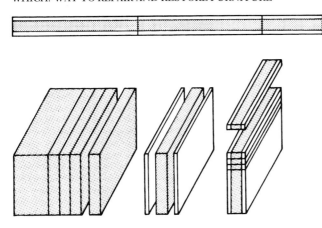

2.26a A simple type of banding. Square off the end of the centre type of wood, and saw sections. Glue the veneer for the outer type of wood to each side, to form a sandwich. Slice the sandwich with a knife or saw, to the thickness required for the banding. Glue the banding in place, building up the length required from the cuttings. Sand or scrape it down to produce a smooth finish.

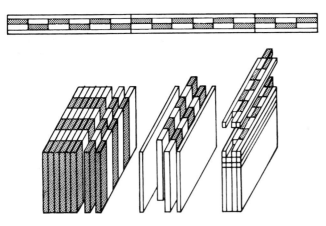

b To produce a chequered banding, glue two types of wood together, and cut segments from the end. Reverse alternate segments, and reglue them, with veneer to form the outer wood. Slice the banding as before.

If lost, clean the recess of old glue and debris, and glue in new stringing or matching banding.

You may be able to buy banding to match exactly the portion that has survived. If not, choose between lifting out all the old wood and replacing it entirely, or making up small pieces of your own banding to an exact match. On valuable antique furniture, the less you replace the better. On less valuable pieces, a complete replacement is often simpler.

If you can buy banding to match, trim the broken end with a sharp chisel and cut the replacement to length with a scalpel.

Glue it in place. Use an offcut to experiment with stains and polishes to produce a finish that matches the old wood. Normal everyday wear and periodic polishing of the whole area will help the woods to blend together.

If replacing the banding completely, lift out the old wood with a chisel. Remove traces of glue from the recess with a hot damp cloth. Mitre the corners when glueing in the new banding, by overlapping one piece with the other and cutting carefully through both with a scalpel, protecting the surrounding wood with waste veneer.

To match unusually patterned bandings you may have to make up your own. First determine what kinds of wood you have to match. Those typically used in banding include satinwood, boxwood for thin pale yellow lines, and ebony for black-and-pale chequered effects.

Take as an example a simple three-strand banding. The main central strand is generally cut across the grain, making the grain visible and giving the surface plenty of character. Start by squaring the end of a piece of wood for the centre strand, as in [2.26a]. Cut a slice off the end to the width of the centre part of the banding. To each side, glue a veneer of the species of wood for the narrow outer strands of the banding. From this 'sandwich', with a fine saw or knife, slice thin sections. Lay them end to end to build up the length of banding required. Any irregularities or excess depth can be sanded away when the banding is in place.

A more complicated but widely used banding consists of a chequered pattern. Start by glueing blocks of two types of wood together. Slice them into segments as thick as half the width of the centre banding. Arrange them in pairs to give a chequered effect [2.26b] and glue them together, with the veneers on the outer side as in the first example. When they are firmly glued, slice off the sections of banding as before.

Stringing is far simpler. A sharp spike is essential to clear the recess of the old stringing. Work a hot damp cloth into it to remove any old glue. Brush new glue into the recess and press the stringing into place, working from one end and forcing it well down into the recess bit by bit. When the glue has completely set, smooth the stringing flush with the surrounding surface, using either a cabinet-maker's scraper or glasspaper.

It is hardly worth making your own stringing, but in case you cannot find a suitable replacement, here is a simple technique. First, plane a piece of the required wood square on all sides. Boxwood is used more often than any other wood for this purpose. Clamp a steel rule to one side,

the same distance from the edge as the thickness of stringing that you require. If you cannot gauge that accurately, cut it slightly over-size. It can be reduced later with glasspaper to give a tight fit when dry.

Clamp the wood in a vice and slice along it against the straight edge with a craft knife or scalpel, keeping both hands well behind the blade for safety. Turn the work on to its side, and clamp the ruler on again. Then make a second cut to meet the first. The stringing should come away cleanly.

Cut one length of stringing off each of the four corners of the wood. You may be able to cut off a second and third length all round. If not, plane the wood square again to give you four fresh corners to work on. There are other methods of producing stringing and you may well devise one that suits you better.

Marquetry

A restoration problem that is in many ways similar to banding occurs in much fine antique furniture. It arises when marquetry pictures become damaged. You may have to replace one part of a picture, or all of it. Bear in mind the general rule of restoration – that the more original an article the more valuable it is. But remember also that any furniture in a good state of repair is more attractive.

Marquetry is similar to inlay. Both consist of veneer, but in marquetry the pattern is made up of several pieces of veneer, assembled into a picture or design then glued into place. Inlay consists of small pieces of veneer let into the recesses in the ground.

To restore a complete picture in marquetry, first draw a reproduction of the original as accurately as possible. You may be able to take it from the remains of the damaged marquetry. If that is unrecognisable, draw up a new picture by referring to a photograph of a similar piece of furniture. Draw the design in a clear thin line and take photocopies of it, one for each of the different woods in the marquetry pattern. Give a number to each of the different woods, and mark the number for one of the woods on each photocopy. Then, referring to the original drawing, mark the number of the wood on each drawing on the separate sections of the picture. From each sheet, cut out the numbered sections roughly with scissors, slightly over-size all round. Paste these parts of the picture on a piece of waste veneer, with the pattern elements for each wood close together. Cut the waste veneer into separate parts – one for each wood – so that you have the pattern elements for each wood on its own piece.

Now make up several 'sandwiches' – again one for each wood. Put the waste veneer with the paper shapes pasted on to it on top. Underneath, lay the fine veneer from which you are going to cut those parts of the pattern. Underneath that you need a sheet of plywood which will support the fine veneer while you cut it. The three parts of the sandwich must be held tightly together, so obtain some veneer pins, nail them right through the sandwich between the paper shapes and bend over the ends. At this stage some skilful fine cutting is called for. Serious woodworking enthusiasts may have a band-saw or power jig-saw to work with. A hand fretsaw is just as good and gives plenty of control. Hold it upright and cut round the outline of the shapes in each drawing [**2.27**]. The pieces of veneer will fall out, cut to exactly the size and shape required for the pattern.

Professional marquetry producers work this way, but put several pieces of fine veneer into each sandwich. Several thicknesses of the same veneer will reproduce the same picture several times. Different types of veneer in each sandwich will produce different versions of the picture.

With all the pieces cut, assemble them on a copy of the original drawing. They should fit exactly, but any adjustments are easy to make with a scalpel or glasspaper. When satisfied with the fit, paste them on to a reverse image of the drawing. You can easily make one of these with carbon paper. And now you can turn the marquetry picture over, and glue it on to the ground. When it is dry, simply wipe off the paper with a damp cloth. Finally sand down and polish the picture.

An interesting variation, which can produce remarkably beautiful marquetry work, involves shading the individual pieces.

Fill an old tobacco tin with fine dry sand. Heat the sandbox over a low flame. Holding the veneer with a pair of tweezers, push it slowly into the sand, about halfway [**2.28**]. When removed, you

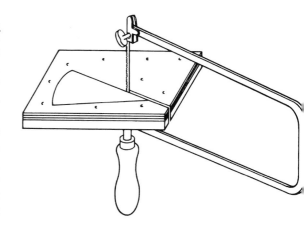

2.27 Cut marquetry pictures with a fine fretsaw, from a sandwich formed from the picture segments, fine veneer and a plywood base.

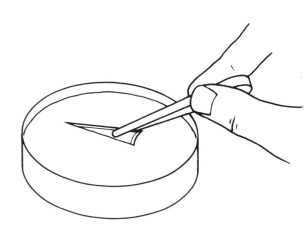

2.28 You can shade pieces of the veneer by dipping the parts into a bed of heated sand, to darken it slightly.

will see that the hot sand has darkened it permanently. If you experiment with offcuts, you can vary the rate at which you push the veneer into the sand, and the time needed to produce perfectly graded shading. Assemble the picture as before and you may be surprised at the quality of the finished piece.

When only parts are missing from a marquetry picture or design, replacing them is similar to repairing veneer. With a soft pencil, make a rubbing of the area to be replaced. Clean out the recess. Make up a sandwich as in marquetry to cut the new piece, and glue it in place.

Making up your own inlay, banding and stringing, and your own marquetry patterns might be considered fiddly work, and may be more interesting to the woodworking enthusiast than to the ordinary householder who simply wants to keep his furniture in good repair.

DISTRESSING

If you have let in a substantial piece, or even replaced a complete member, you will have a fine new part looking startlingly out of character with the old. Its faces will be smooth, its edges sharp and true. In the reproduction industry, the process of making a newly manufactured article of furniture look as if it has been in use for a couple of hundred years is called 'distressing'.

It is perhaps advisable to opt for a complete concealment in restoration, and simulate the kind of damage the rest of the piece has suffered. The first thing to do is sand down the sharp edges, to reproduce the wear that any furniture will have suffered in years of use.

Around handles and door edges, the hundreds of tiny indentations that fingernails make can be simulated by tapping the surface for a few minutes with a wire egg whisk. Go over the surface lightly and fast as if beating a drum roll.

A device frequently used in the trade to reproduce bumps and bruises on old furniture is chain. A short length of fairly heavy chain, with about one-inch links, will make the right kind of shallow marks in a random pattern. Some distressers make up a kind of 'cat o'nine tails' with three lengths of chain attached to a handle. You can probably achieve equally realistic damage by dropping the chain a couple of feet on to your new wood.

An alternative is to tap the wood with a rough selection of tools – hammers, screwdrivers, chisels – in random fashion. You will soon have the new wood looking as worn as the original.

METAL REPAIRS

Faults to the metal parts of furniture may form only a small part of the amateur restorer's work, and many people who are enthusiasts for wood and its working take less pleasure in dealing with metal. Nevertheless, it can be extremely difficult and expensive to find professional craftsmen prepared to do the work, and there is no reason to avoid this aspect of restoration. The tools are similar, and the operations run on the same basic lines – dismantling, removing damaged or worn material and replacing it with new, reassembly, and polishing.

Handles

If it is not possible to find a matching example in an antique shop, a reproduction is probably the only answer. It may be possible to buy a similar item slightly too big and alter it to produce an exact match. Brass plate can be filed quite easily and sawn with a hacksaw. If a swan-neck handle is oversize, you can easily reduce it, and this kind of exercise serves as a good starting experience for working in metal. The technique is similar to woodwork, but first you must anneal the brass. Heat it in a gas flame, then plunge it into cold water. It will lose any brittleness and become workable.

Cut out the excess and file down the mating parts to the same diameter. If the faces meet well, you can solder them together without difficulty. On a repair of this size, the best heat source is a modern butane-gas blowlamp. Nozzles come in various grades for the bottled-gas blowlamp, and one which produces a fine flame will suit this kind of work.

First, file the faces smooth and coat them with soldering flux. Fix the parts in a vice, with the faces touching, and play the blowlamp flame over the joint until the area heats up. Now take a length of solder (it comes either on a spool or on a card), remove the heat source and touch the solder to the join while the brass is still hot. The solder will melt and run into the joint by capillary attraction, and will seal itself to the two brass faces wherever you applied the flux. File away any odd spots of solder and polish the brass.

This is not the strongest of joints. Other ways of working metal such as brazing and welding give a far stronger bond, but are beyond the scope of the average amateur restorer. Even so, the solder should be strong enough to hold the handle together, and if you have worked with precision, nobody should see the join when the renewed handle is on display.

Locks

The problem is usually that the key is missing. The restorer with average skill will find it easy to cut one to fit. If the cabinet was locked when the key disappeared it may be possible to take out other drawers to gain access to the screws that hold the lock, or to prise apart a weak cabinet to gain access.

Locks made before 1778 were relatively simple, and it may be possible to make a key that will open one. Once the lock is open, dismantle it and cut a new, more accurate key with a saw and file.

Whether or not a key will turn in this type of lock depends on it matching a set of obstacles called 'wards'. If the slots in the key let it pass the wards, it will operate the bolt. The wards were simply fixed to the sides of the lock casing.

First obtain a blank that will fit the lock. A few minutes careful measuring, probing and estimating will give you the length and depth of the key flange and the diameter of the pin over which the stem of the key fits. Then hunt out a good locksmith or ironmonger who stocks blanks of the right size. Buy at least two – one for experimenting and one for a finished job.

Mix up a paste from petroleum jelly and some dark colouring pigment, such as powder paint. Spread a thin layer on the key flange and start to turn it in the lock. The obstacles it encounters should show up as clear indentations in the layer of jelly. Mark them with a file and with the key blank held firmly in a vice, cut them out with a hacksaw and file.

A series of inventions after 1778 introduced a variety of locking systems, with tumblers, levers and cylinders – each more complicated, more ingenious, and more secure than the last. Most of them are too tricky to pick or unlock from the outside, and you will have to remove the lock and dismantle it [2.29]. Once the lock is open and you can see the inner mechanical parts, it is possible to reproduce the key that will open it, and to replace worn parts to bring the lock back to working order. But this is advanced-level metalwork, comparable in difficulty to car mechanics.

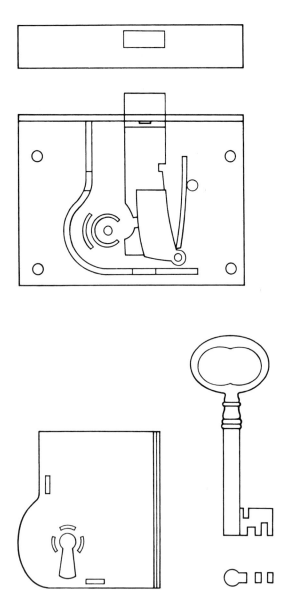

2.29   It is possible to cut a key to pass the 'wards' that protect early locks.

Inlaid brass

Inlaid brass occasionally causes problems, as the glue weakens and corners lift, frequently helped by wood shrinkage or even an over-enthusiastic duster. If the trouble is simply a raised corner, ease some adhesive under it and hold it down until it has set.

Take care in repairing brass inlay. It is thin material and liable to crease permanently if it is folded. Do not try to pull it back to lift it. Instead, slide a thin wooden wedge under it and prise it away from its bed. If the wooden base has shrunk it may be necessary to cut a small piece out of the brass, so that later it drops easily back into place.

When all the old glue is cleaned out of the recess, stick the inlay down. Using a modern adhesive which bonds equally well with wood or metal, make up a form of caul to press the inlay home firmly until the glue has set. Some restorers use pins to help keep the brass in place.

The thinnest brass-wire tapered pins should be used. While glueing in the inlay, hammer the pins gently through the brass until they penetrate the wood beneath and hold the inlay down. When the bond has set firm, nip off the protruding ends of the pins with pincers and sandpaper the whole area flush. When you polish the finished work the pins will not show.

3 Cleaning, stripping and refinishing

Some of the furniture in your home will have nothing seriously wrong with it and there will be no reason to carry out any structural repairs or restoration. But many pieces in otherwise sound condition would benefit from careful cleaning.

The finishing processes described in this chapter are designed so that you can work out as you go just how radical a treatment your furniture needs. They start with a simple cleaning process and move on in stages to a complete strip down and refinishing.

If you follow this sequence you will gain practical experience of refinishing, without damaging the furniture you are working on. If there is a finish worth preserving under several layers of grime and sooty deposit, you will be able to recover it in a few hours of careful work.

Working by stages in this way is a great advantage to the beginner in restoration. By the time you have completed a few pieces of your own, you will have less need to go through the processes one by one, and you will be able to judge exactly what is needed from the look and feel of the piece.

Broadly speaking, finishes fall into two categories. 'Hard' finishes coat the wood in a fine protective shell. They include French polish, shellac, and various kinds of varnishes and lacquers. So long as they remain unscratched, they should protect the wood from dirt and remain impervious to dirt themselves. Other finishes might be called 'soft'. The main one is wax polish, prepared according to a variety of recipes. Wax is a fine finish and tough enough to ward off ordinary dirt. Eventually, however, it loses its freshness and gathers grime.

Until recently, rooms were warmed mainly by coal fires which wafted particles of dust and smoke into the atmosphere. Over the years, some wooden furniture got so badly blackened that the grain and character of the wood became invisible.

The best article to start cleaning, then, is the blackest and dullest piece of furniture you can find. If the finish is wax, you will soon reveal the wood beneath. If it is black for some other reason – black lacquer for example – your cleaning will have no effect and you can go on to the next step.

REVIVERS

'Reviver' is the trade term for a solution used to improve the wax finish on wood. It is possible to buy revivers, but perfectly simple to make up your own. Recipes for revivers were once closely guarded trade secrets. Now they are freely available.

The simplest are generally effective, but it is worth experimenting with the more complicated ones if you can obtain the ingredients. The simplest recipe of all is a mixture of vinegar and water, though water can have a slightly unhappy effect on wood through 'lifting' the grain. Vinegar by itself – or at least the acetic acid in it – can be a moderately effective way of cutting through grease. But more effective on most surfaces is a concoction known as 'half-and-half'. It consists of equal quantities of raw linseed oil and turps substitute (white spirit). Then a third ingredient is added – a dash of vinegar.

An eggcupful of each of the two main ingredients produces enough reviver to clean the average piece of furniture. Mix them up in a bottle and shake well before and during use, otherwise the vinegar will separate out.

Make a note of the recipe for future reference. *Label the bottle clearly and keep well out of reach of children.*

Use 'half-and-half' on dirty furniture, work it round and round with a soft cloth such as muslin. Wipe the surface with a clean cloth, and repeat as often as you continue to get results. Use an old toothbrush to reach difficult corners, mouldings and carvings.

Often, treatment with a reviver is all a piece needs to bring it back to life. The grain shows again, and you can maintain the condition by simple polishing.

Precisely how the reviver works depends on the nature of the dirt you are trying to dislodge. Basically the acetic acid cuts through the grease, the white spirit dissolves at least the top layer of polish, and the linseed oil, as well as lubricating the whole process, seeps down through the polish and feeds the wood. Then it dries to help give a hard shine. A word of caution: when linseed oil sinks into wood it darkens it considerably. If your furniture is dark enough already, you may want to avoid this. More important, your layers of polish may not be even. If it is cracked or patchy, the oil will affect some parts more than others, leaving a permanent skewbald effect. If you are working on a cracked French polish surface, the oil will seep into the cracks and can leave a permanent and indelible stain recording exactly where the cracks were. Some restorers will not allow linseed oil near furniture, unless they are using it all over.

Some polishers use methylated spirits instead of turps substitute. One recipe recommends equal parts of raw linseed oil, methylated spirits and vinegar. Another gives only two parts methylated spirits, to 48 parts vinegar and 50 parts raw linseed oil. Clearly you can vary the exact measures to suit yourself. They seem to make little difference to the way the basic mix works.

Several other well-established recipes use more obscure ingredients. If you can buy them somewhere, you may like to experiment with them. Here are two:

1   1 cupful vinegar
     1 cupful methylated spirits
     1oz camphor
     1oz raw linseed oil
     ½oz butter of antimony

2   4 parts raw linseed oil
     12 parts vinegar
     1 part terebene

Wire wool

Applied with a cloth, the reviver may not produce the desired finish. It may be that the wax has flaked off in parts and has become patchy, in which case you will have to remove it all. The dirt may be particularly stubborn, neither muslin nor any other cloth will be strong enough to dislodge it with any of the revivers.

If so, go on to the next stage in the cleaning process and use one of the furniture restorer's most useful items, wire wool. This is available in five grades: 5 is the most coarse; the finest is 000. Most hardware stores stock only the medium grades, but you will need the finest for several operations in furniture finishing, so it is worth asking your local shop to order you a supply. Specialist polish suppliers stock it in all grades. Buy plenty at a time; you will be using and discarding it in fairly large amounts.

Try rubbing in a reviver with wire wool. Work with a featherlight touch at first, and the wire wool may take off just enough of the dirty and greasy surface to leave a finish of serviceable old polish. If results are slow in coming, increase the pressure but not enough to scratch the wood. Work round and round until the dirt begins to loosen, then finish with long smooth strokes along the length of the grain to clean out any dirt trapped there.

When the wire wool gets clogged, turn it to produce a clean surface, and when it is full of debris discard it altogether and make a new pad.

A stronger alternative is to use wire wool with methylated spirits alone as a solvent. When you finally wipe off the debris from the surface you may reveal an adequately restored finish without expending too much time or effort.

If none of these methods succeeds, it could mean that the finish is some form of cellulose.

Now try cellulose thinner with wire wool. Make sure you open the windows because thinner gives off potentially dangerous vapours. Wear rubber gloves and give the surface to be stripped a wash with the thinner, or a mixture of thinner and methylated spirits. Experiment to find the most effective proportions for the surface concerned, and work quickly, because thinner soon evaporates. Keep rubbing and applying the solvent until the surface layers are reduced to a sticky paste. Wipe this away and give the surface a final wash down with a rag soaked in methylated spirits.

If the surface is too tough to respond to any of these treatments, or if you are confident you can do better by starting all over again, strip it back to bare wood.

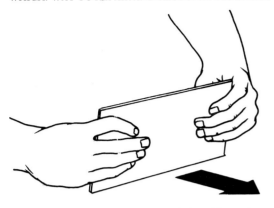

3.1 Use the scraper with a two-handed pushing action to strip a plain surface.

STRIPPING

In recent years the widespread practice has developed of stripping wood, particularly pine, by immersing it in a bath of caustic soda. This rapidly removes all finishes, including paint. The method is fine for kitchen furniture but too brutal for good items, leaving as it does, a grey lifeless surface, and obscuring the grain.

The owner who cares for his furniture, and has the time and patience to work on it, must use more discriminating techniques. The aim is to take off the top layers of dirt and polish, leaving the lower layers intact, and not affecting the wood itself. This will also save several stages of work in re-polishing.

Using a scraper

First take off as much of the unwanted finish as possible by purely mechanical means. The best tool for this is a cabinet-maker's scraper (see page 14).

Hold the scraper in both hands with the sharp hook away from you, the fingers wrapped round behind it, and the thumbs nearest you. Now push it away from you in the direction of the grain [3.1]. A few strokes with the scraper will remove all the unwanted material. Do not allow the scraper to lean over at the edge of a surface. This puts a bevel on the corners and can cut right through a thin veneer.

Scraping off layers of old polish may leave the surface smooth enough for refinishing. But the scraper only works on relatively flat surfaces. On turned work, or on concave parts of the furniture, you will have to apply a stripping solvent.

Strippers

It is essential to use a stripper that is spirit-based. Water-based strippers remove the unwanted finish but washing down the bare wood with water may 'raise the grain'. You can see this effect on a piece of untreated softwood after it has been soaked: it looks and feels slightly fluffy, and loses its hard smooth surface even when dry. If this happens with furniture you will have to re-smooth it with a scraper or glasspaper. You will also find you have dislodged any grain filler that the original craftsman used. In fact, you will have to start further back in the process than is necessary or advisable.

The containers used for commercial strippers may not state whether the contents are water-based or spirit-based. The clue can be found in the directions for use. If they advise washing down with water, the stripper is water-based; if with methylated spirits or white spirits, they are spirit-based.

Wearing rubber gloves, apply the stripper with a brush. As soon as the top layer dissolves and bubbles up to form a loose dirty paste, clear it away. Use an ordinary paint scraper in the early stages on accessible surfaces. In the later stages and where you cannot manipulate the scraper, use wire wool.

After each application wipe over the surface with a rag or cotton wool pad well soaked in methylated spirits. Work quickly, to prevent the solvent penetrating too deeply. You may be able to stop stripping before the solvent attacks the lower layers of the polish, or the original bodying-in of the grain, or affects the colouring of the wood itself. All these will have remained unaffected by the dirt and grease of decades of use, and form an ideal ready-made base layer for your new finish.

Make sure you wash all surfaces well with liberal applications of methylated spirits to give yourself scrupulously clean and grease-free furniture to re-start polishing.

Removing ring marks

Ring marks commonly occur on table-tops either through spilling hot liquids and alcohol or from the dry heat of dishes straight from the oven.

Proprietary removers are generally quite cheap and easy to use. They do a good job of eliminating

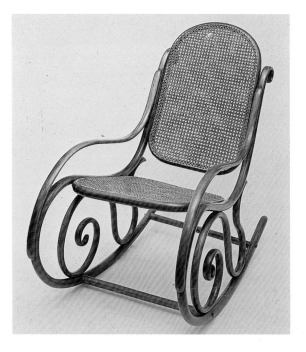

Above: a stuffed-over seat showing a close-nailed effect finish.

Above: a bentwood rocking-chair with cane seat and back.

Below: two ebonised wood chairs with cane seat and back panels.

Above: a dismantled chair ready for restoration, with two 5′ sash cramps and softwood pads in position. Beneath the chair is a selection of tools used by the furniture restorer. *(L to R)* 10″ smoothing plane, 1″ chisel, ½″ chisel, bradawl, cross-pein hammer, ¼″ chisel, 7″ smoothing plane, 6″ G-cramp.

Various styles of chair *Above left:* a Windsor chair. *Below (L to R):* an Edwardian chair, with padded seat and back in a show-wood frame; the padding is edged with decorative braid. A wickerwork chair with a separate padded cushion. Nineteenth-century armchair with stuffed-over seat, padded arms and braid trim.

Above: detail from a nineteenth-century walnut chair showing the vulnerable join of the curved top rail and curved back upright.

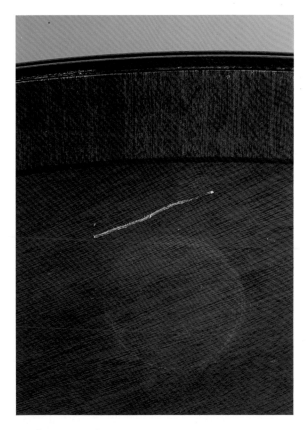

Repairs to wood surfaces *Above left:* a wooden table-top with a scratch mark and a stain ring left by a coffee cup on the surface. *Above right:* the surface after repair by proprietary removers and fillers.

Below left and right: a yew-wood stool, and a chest of drawers with badly worn surface.

Opposite page: the sequence of stages involved in transforming an old painted kitchen chair. *L to R, top to bottom:* the application of a proprietary stripper to remove the layers of paint. Filling of cracks in the stripped-down chair with a wood filler. Sanding down the arm to prepare the base for the stain or varnish. Application of stain to the prepared wood.

Left: a wreck of an armchair before the restoration process begins. In this instance, the armchair must be dismantled down to the bare frame. The wooden feet have been protected against damage.

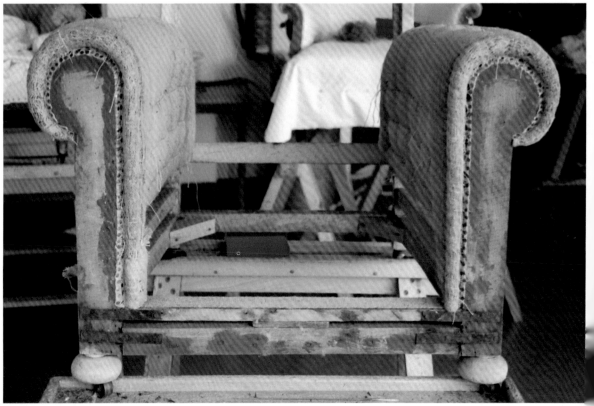

Opposite, top right: the dismantling process has begun. This picture reveals the intricate patterns of springing and webbing to be found in the back of an armchair once the back cover has been removed. When you are dismantling an armchair like this, it is advisable to make a sketch or take a photograph of the sewing, springing and webbing arrangements to remind you how to do it as you build up the armchair from scratch.

Left: the padded scrolled arms of the armchair. You can clearly see the through-stuffing ties on the inside of each arm, the padding over the top of the arms and the hessian held in place with a series of tacks.

Above: the scroll back of the armchair with its cover in place, awaiting the covered scroll front to be attached. The picture shows the pleated material around the scroll with the pleats pointing down to a central point. The length of piping cord, in the same material, can be seen hanging from the back of the arm.

Above: a Victorian button-back chair with braid trim.

Above left: detail from a button-back chair showing the hard-edge construction, through-stuffing ties and tacks in place prior to the deep-buttoning stage.

Left: the finished button-back chair with buttoning extending towards the arms.

Above: an upholstered medallion-back chair in a show-wood frame.

Right: an example of close-nailing as a decorative border around the front and back of this padded sofa.

Pine furniture *Above left:* a pine chest of drawers.
For an explanation of how to repair drawers, see page
34; for replacing metal handles, see page 43. *Above
right:* a pine kitchen chair, *below left:* a pine kitchen
table. For an explanation of how to repair a table-top,
see page 30. *Below right:* a pine ladderback chair
with a simple drop-in seat.

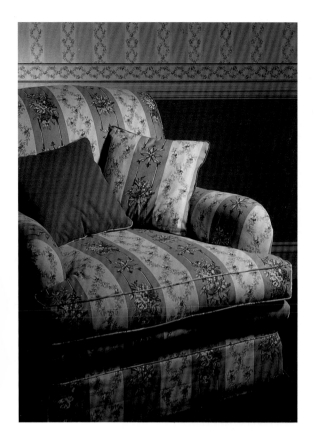

Above left and right: comfortable armchairs with T-shaped cushions and piping cord effect around the seams.

Right: a refurbished sofa showing many restoration skills: scrolled arms, padded cushions and piping cord.

A wing armchair upholstered in linen, with piping cord in the same fabric running around the outer and inner edges of the arms.

marks, but the main problem is that they also polish the surface to a gloss – all right on a table which already has a deep shine, but conspicuous on a matt or semi-matt table.

It is possible to dull down the gloss by rubbing in builders' chalk with linseed oil. However, it is very difficult to regain the original finish, especially in direct comparison with the surrounding undamaged area.

Most manufacturers instruct you to apply their product with a soft cloth and this would seem more sensible than tipping remover directly on to the wood, particularly when it's French polished or highly waxed – the types of finish which might dissolve too readily, leaving you with the added problem of an uneven surface.

When using a remover, remember the following:

wear protective gloves
keep it well away from children and naked flames
always rub in line with the grain
test on a hidden area of the table first.

Three home remedies, also applied with a soft cloth, are:
'half-and-half' reviver (see page 46)
metal polish
methyl alcohol.

Of these, metal polish works as well as proprietary removers, but this too leaves the surface glossy. Methyl alcohol does not produce a gloss, however it is *extremely* powerful and can damage the table without sufficient care. It's also hard to find because chemists can sell it only if they have a special licence.

Depending on the type of mark and the nature of the surface, you may have to be prepared to strip and refinish the whole table-top, perhaps with a robust oil finish (see page 51).

Filling scratches

There are two types of product available for mending a scratch. One is a liquid that stains the exposed wood. The other is a coloured wax stick that is rubbed into the scratch to fill it. You will probably obtain the best result by judicious combination of the two.

Colour matching is notoriously difficult, expect to be obliged to mix colours, especially if the scratch goes across the grain. Some manufacturers of wax sticks actually sell boxes of assorted colours so that you can experiment until satisfied.

So, first stain the bare wood with a liquid. The scratch 'profile' will almost certainly still be visible. Fill the damaged area with plenty of wax, then take a straight edge (like a credit card) and scrape off the excess cleanly. This seems to work better than rubbing it with a cloth which tends to lift some of the wax out of the scratch again.

The acceptability of the result depends on the colour match and of course, on the position of the scratch. You could take the remedy further than the wax filling, by smoothing the wax with fine garnet paper lubricated with linseed oil and then painting it with a spirit colour mixed with French polish. If the scratch is still too obvious, stripping and refinishing the entire surface may be the only solution.

Removing ink stains

Ink stains on wood are almost inevitable on any antique desk or bureau.

They are easy to remove using oxalic acid which you should be able to obtain through your local chemist. *Oxalic acid is highly poisonous*, so lock it away when not in use. The chemist sells it in the form of crystals. Dissolve two tablespoonsful in 30–50mls of water in the bottom of a bottle. *Label the bottle clearly and keep well out of reach of children.*

Wear rubber gloves. Pour the acid generously over the stained area to form a small pool. Dab it in with a wad of cotton wool for a few minutes, then soak up the acid with a dry wad. Repeat the process. It may take an hour or so of dabbing and washing, but eventually the old ink will be neutralised and the stain will disappear.

The treatment can change the colour of the wood slightly in the area where the acid has been applied. Pale mahogany, for example, turns from a yellow to a slightly pink shade, so once the ink stain has gone, wash the acid lightly over the whole surface. The colour may not be all the same, but the edges of the treated area will be less noticeable.

Some restorers recommend hydrogen peroxide, or ordinary household bleach, but these leave a distinct patch which you will have to re-stain to match the surrounding wood.

REFINISHING

Wherever you have let in new segments of wood, or replaced complete members, the furniture will require a new finish.

Many craftsmen find refinishing the most satisfying part of all furniture restoration though the process can be rather bewildering as well as satisfying for the beginner. Even when you have worked out which finish is ideal for your piece of furniture, according to the age of the piece, its value and its future use, you will still find almost as many methods of applying each finish as there are polishers trained in the craft.

For the best results you should concentrate at first on a limited range of processes. That way you may get enough practice to achieve a finish virtually indistinguishable from that of a professional polisher. Once you have acquired a measure of skill, you can go on to experiment with some of the more unusual methods.

There are three basic steps in finishing. First, colouring the wood: in the case of most restoration work attempting the difficult task of matching new wood to old. Second, filling in the grain ready to take the final polish. Lastly, giving the final polish, both to enhance the appearance and to protect the wood from damage in use.

Staining

When you have let in new wood or made a new part for an item of furniture, you will have wood which is a different colour from the surrounding material. And when you have stripped or scraped an area, it will almost certainly need re-colouring back to its original shade.

Old texts list the chemicals used on various species of wood to achieve all the colours and tones that the restorer might require. The problem that home craftsmen face today is that these materials are becoming increasingly difficult to obtain in their raw state. Specialist manufacturers can supply them, but they are designed mainly for the professional cabinet-maker or polisher who will economise by being able to mix up large quantities of any stain he needs from the basic raw materials.

Proprietary stains and wood dyes are quite adequate for the home restorer, who will have only small quantities of wood to colour.

A thimbleful is generally enough to colour a chair leg and an eggcupful will completely cover a new table-top. So the cost of materials for this work is relatively low, and the convenience of being able to buy from the local d-i-y store gives them the advantage over cheaper but more complicated chemicals bought from a specialist.

However there is one pitfall. For restoration purposes, the names on the tins are meaningless. Proprietory stains are made for colouring pale softwoods such as pine and deal to make them look like the more interesting hardwoods. Although the grain is unlikely to be convincing, you can stain a pine table with a mahogany colour and to the uninitiated it will look more or less like a mahogany table.

If, on the other hand, you have let a piece of mahogany into the leg of a table to make a repair, staining it with a mahogany stain will have quite a different effect. It might even turn it bright red.

The technique, as always, is to test on an offcut of the wood you are using. And you should achieve the right colour by mixing two or more stains.

Buy three tins or bottles of stain in the first instance. 'Medium oak' will give a standard brown colour, 'mahogany' will give a redder shade, and 'walnut' will give a slightly greyer, flatter tone. From these three you should be able to produce a good match to most woods commonly used in furniture.

To estimate the effects of mixing any two or all three stains, make a chart; any piece of white-wood board will do. On it, mark a large square and sub-divide that into nine smaller ones. With a small pad made from a square of cloth wrapped round a wad of cotton wool, apply the stain neat to the first three squares. Label them clearly.

Next mix the stains in pairs in equal quantities. A few drops in a bottle-top will be plenty. Apply the mixes on the second row and label them. On the bottom row make up a mixture of all three. That will leave two squares, on which to experiment with different quantities, or with diluted versions. White spirits is a good dilutant but check if any other is specified on the tin or bottle.

If you buy four cans of stain, you will need ten squares, and if you buy five, fifteen squares. You will probably find that some of the squares are very similar. And remember that you are experimenting on white wood, which will produce a different effect from the wood used in your work.

In the end you should be able to produce, quite quickly, the mix to give the right colour for your final wood. Test it first on the offcut.

Remember also that when you are staining end-grain, it absorbs more and shows up considerably darker than the sides and edges. So either dilute the stain, or apply fewer coats.

Filling

Before applying stain to your wood, you have to consider whether you need to fill the grain or not. An open-grained wood like oak can be attractive with the grain left unfilled. Any stain will tend to accumulate in the grain, leaving it slightly darker. Any wax or polish will build up in the recess and form an effective filler.

In French polishing, the first application of polish fills most of the pores in the wood, and subsequent applications build up a hard surface so that no filler is necessary. The disadvantage is that this process takes time, and professionals like to use a filling material to shorten the early stages.

If you want to do the same, filling is a simple operation. The best and most convenient filler is plaster of Paris, but it is glaring white, so you will have to add a colour to prevent it showing through.

The best material for colouring plaster is Vandyke brown powder paint. Mix into the plaster, using just enough to take away the whiteness for light woods, and more for dark woods.

To apply the filler, dab a damp cloth pad into the plaster so that it picks up a deposit, and rub it in circular movements over the workpiece. Before the plaster begins to set, lift the residue from the surface of the work by wiping it *across* the grain with a clean cloth.

If there are larger holes to be filled, for example an old screw hole, or a bruise that refuses to come out with the damp heat treatment described on page 38, a more substantial form of stopping will be needed.

Several proprietary products are available, such as plastic wood, in a variety of shades to match surrounding wood. Work them in with a spatula or putty knife, and sand them level when dry.

An alternative filler is stick stopping, which looks like sealing wax, and again is available in various shades from specialist polish manufacturers.

Melt the wax with a hot iron (an old screwdriver heated in a gas flame will do) directly over the fault to be filled. The wax will drip into place. Level it with a scraper when it has set. To help fix the filler in place, prick the recessed area several times with a pin before melting in the wax. The wax will then penetrate the holes and form a set of 'roots'.

Oil finish

Oil finishing takes time, a lot of hard work, and demands long intervals between applications, but it is an excellent finish for much domestic furniture. It stands up well to ordinary household treatment. Hot plates, spilled liquids and scratches do little harm; and if it should need repair, it is simple to rub in a new coating.

Providing you can leave the piece out of commission for several weeks, and have the patience to wait for each application to dry, oil is the easiest finish to apply.

First choose a stain that is several shades lighter than the colour you finally want, as the oil will darken the wood.

Then rub in a light coating of linseed oil. Rub until the oil goes dry. Repeat after a few days. Eventually you will build up an attractive eggshell sheen.

Polishing experts are equally divided over which oil you should use – boiled linseed or raw linseed oil.

Boiled linseed oil will dry in about twenty-four hours and you can then apply the next coat.

You can produce your own boiled oil. Simmer raw oil for fifteen minutes and add one part turpentine to eight parts of the linseed oil, plus terebine to help the drying, in the proportion of one teaspoonful to a half-pint.

Raw linseed oil takes up to three days to dry (some experts recommend leaving it for a month), but once it is dry it produces a harder surface.

On balance, it is recommended for the person who can afford to wait long intervals between coats.

Apply the linseed oil with a cloth or pad of wadding. Give the surface just a thin coating. Rub it in well. Some polishers use a brick or heavy wood block, covered in felt or velvet, to increase the pressure.

Leave the job until the oil dries. Repeat the process every few days, for up to a month if possible, to build up a good hard coating. You could go on indefinitely. Applying the occasional coat of oil over the years keeps the wood in good order. It is comforting to know that you can do little damage to this kind of surface that is not quickly and easily put right.

An alternative technique is to apply a mixture of equal parts of linseed oil and turpentine for the initial coat. Brush it on thinly, rub it lightly, and leave it for a month. The coats that follow should contain a higher proportion of linseed oil, and each one should be left for several weeks to harden completely. This is a slow process, but it gives a satisfying, deep polish.

Wax finish

Wax polishing was used long before the introduction of French polishing in the nineteenth century. Wax is therefore an appropriate finish for earlier furniture – oak chairs, oak gate-legged tables, old oak or walnut bureaus and chests. It gives a less glossy surface than French polish, without being dull, and many people prefer it. If applied correctly it produces an attractive sheen which brings out the figuring of the wood.

First stain the wood to the colour required. It is not absolutely necessary to apply any filler. The wax itself will fill the cavities and crevices in the grain, but you might want to use a coloured filler on some open-grained woods such as oak and mahogany, to produce an 'antique' effect.

Before waxing, brush on one, or preferably two, thin coats of white or clear French polish (see page 53 for an explanation of these terms). This simply seals the wood so that it does not absorb the wax. If it did, the dirt would eventually work its way through the wax and into the wood. Clear French polish will not have any appreciable effect on the colour of the wood itself. White polish may darken it slightly.

The piece is now ready for waxing. Either choose one of the proprietary waxes or mix your own. This is easy and some people find it satisfying to go right back to basics. You also know that the ingredients are pure.

Proprietary waxes are available coloured or clear. The coloured ones are designed, as a short cut, to give an antique effect on unstained wood in a single process. You will have more control over your finish if you keep the staining and waxing stages separate.

To mix your own wax, buy a quantity of pure beeswax and a bottle of pure turpentine.

Place the wax in a container – an old shoe polish tin, well cleaned out, is ideal. Place this in a shallow dish of hot water and add enough turpentine to make a half-and-half mixture. When the heat from the water has warmed the ingredients, mix them together. Then let the mixture cool and set. It should be the consistency of a thick paste. The exact proportions of wax to turpentine are not critical. The turps serves only as a vehicle and will eventually evaporate away. Keep the tin of wax sealed when you are not using it.

Professional polishers mix their wax in a double-boiler, the water simmering in the outer container rapidly melts the wax in the inner vessel. You may be able to devise a similar arrangement. *Remember that turpentine is highly inflammable, and heating it over an open flame carries a serious fire risk.*

Make sure that the wood is dry, and, if possible, work in a warm room so that the wax will take well. For the first application, spread the wax sparingly on to the surface with either a cloth or a scrubbing brush – a brush is essential for carvings and cavities.

Polish the wax with a soft cloth and leave it to harden for a few days before applying the second coat.

The wax finish does not keep out dirt as well as French polish. But it is a simple matter, if dirt and dust are absorbed over the years, to clean the surface with an application of half-and-half reviver and apply a new coat of wax.

An alternative recipe uses carnauba wax. This hardens the polish and improves its protective qualities. A well-proven recipe consists of

four parts beeswax
five parts turpentine
one part carnauba wax.

Shred the carnauba wax with a knife before mixing it.

To keep the finish in good order, dust it off occasionally, and every couple of months apply a very fine coating of wax. One wipe of the cloth across the top of your tin of wax should be enough to polish a large piece of furniture, or two or three small ones.

French polishing

French polishing is without doubt the most challenging finish for both the professional and the amateur. It is not really suitable for furniture which will be in heavy use – dining chairs and tables suffer too much rough treatment to carry a finish which is vulnerable to heat and scratches – but for decorative furniture such as side tables, bureaus, hall chairs or library tables it is perfect.

French polish is a generic name for a range of finishing liquids made from shellac dissolved in a solvent, generally alcohol. It is applied in stages, and eventually builds up a hard shell-like layer which gives the wood a deep shine. Shellac itself is an encrustation surrounding an insect, *Lacciffer Lacca*, which lives as a parasite on trees in the Far East.

French polish comes in five basic versions:
French polish is the standard type.
Garnet polish is a darker version made from garnet shellac instead of flake shellac. It gives a deep warm brown finish and is suitable for oak and mahogany.
Button polish is made from shellac in the form of 75mm diameter buttons. It gives a harder finish than standard French polish, but also produces a slightly orange effect. It is therefore useful for heightening the colour of golden-toned woods such as walnut. It is unsuitable for use over dark stains since it tends to obscure the grain.
White polish is made from bleached shellac. Because of its manufacturing process it does not dry as quickly as ordinary French polish. It has roughly the same darkening effect as water.
Clear or transparent polish is made from shellac which has been both bleached and de-waxed. It has the least darkening effect of all. It is useful for sealing very pale woods like pine before waxing.

It is possible to mix your own French polish using shellac and de-natured alcohol or turpentine. But, like most materials used in furniture restoration, the polish is not expensive, and in the quantities likely to be used by the amateur restorer it is advisable to buy manufactured brands.

Specialist suppliers make up various coloured French polishes, for example black and red. They are no longer common, and outside London and one or two other major cities, polishers will have to rely on d-i-y outlets and ironmongers stocking products from one or two main factories. They are unlikely to stock unusual polishes and you will have to achieve the effect you want by staining the wood and applying the polish separately. Test your finish first on an offcut of similar wood, or failing that, on an unobtrusive part of the furniture.

Applying French polish is not difficult, but there are degrees of sophistication which you can achieve with practice. The more advanced are only necessary when working on valuable antique furniture.

Once you have stained the wood satisfactorily and applied any grain filler you want to use, the three basic steps are: *fadding, bodying* and *finishing*.

For successful French polishing, you will have to arrange certain workshop conditions. It is important to work at a reasonably warm temperature, and in fairly dry conditions. Central heating, with a temperature above 65 degrees Fahrenheit (18 degrees Celsius) and all the dampness taken out of the air, produces the ideal atmosphere. If you have to work in an unheated outdoor workshed, you will have to confine your French polishing to the period from late spring to early autumn in the British Isles, unless you can arrange an effective heating system. In hot climates humid summer conditions are often quite unsuitable for French polishing.

Try to arrange your workbench so that it stands between you and the light. You will spend some time looking along the workpiece to pick up reflections, and this is impossible if the light is behind you.

First make a rubber. You will need a chunk of cotton wool big enough to fill the palm of your hand and a piece of cotton or linen cloth about 230mm square. Lawn is an ideal material. It must be white, so that no dyes seep on to the work, and it must be plain, because any fancy textures can leave the imprint of their pattern on the work. Old cotton or linen white shirts are ideal, as are men's white handkerchiefs. The weave should

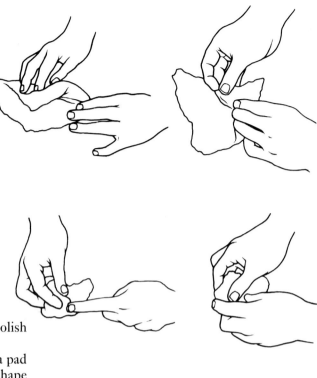

not be too open, or it will allow too much polish to pass through.

Carefully fold the cotton wool [3.2] into a pad with a pointed end and a flat side. Aim for a shape like a pumice stone. The inside of the pad should be fairly big when dry, because soaking it with polish will make it shrink considerably.

Pummel it against your hand and on a table-top to give consistent hardness and a roughly satisfactory shape, place it face down in the middle of the square of material, and gather up the corners to make a small bag. Work it carefully to preserve the pointed end. (The point is for getting the polish into tight corners.)

Now twist up the neck of bag. With your fore-finger on the pointed end, the body of the pad should fall comfortably between your thumb and second finger.

Next, carefully open out the pad on your palm, so as to expose the cotton wool. Try not to dis-turb its shape or put creases on the face. Pour a good dash of French polish into the middle of the cotton wool. Later you will need only the smallest quantity to charge the rubber, but for the first fill-ing you can be fairly generous. Fold the rubber into shape again and dab it on a hard flat surface such as a tile or a sheet of glass.

Dab until the polish feeds out through the front of the rubber on to the flat surface. If none appears, open the rubber and add more polish.

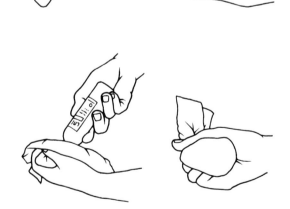

3.2 Fold a chunk of cotton wool into a pear-shaped pad with one flat face. Enclose it in a square of cotton and give the neck a twist. To charge the rubber, open up the neck and pour a generous dash of French polish into the cotton wool.

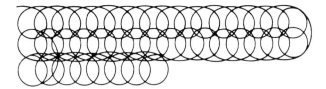

3.3 Apply the polish with a circular action, working in overlapping lines.

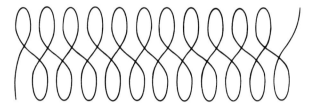

3.4 Vary the pattern with large, even, figure-of-eight movements.

During the polishing process, you will be using controlled pressure from your fingers to feed the polish at the required rate out of the cotton wool, through the weave of the cloth and on to the workpiece itself.

Once polish appears through the face of the rubber as you dab it, you have enough polish in the cotton wool.

Expert French polishers have some variations. For the initial application of polish – the first 'fad' – they do not use a rubber. Instead they fold a piece of wadding into a similar shape, soak it in polish, leave it to dry, soften it again with methylated spirits, and apply the polish using the wadding without a rag cover. They call this wadding pad a 'fad', to distinguish it from the 'rubber' which has the cloth cover. The professional system is designed to save time, but for the home polisher the practice of using a rubber for the first application is perfectly satisfactory.

Put your rubber in a tin or jar with an airtight lid whenever you are not using it. Making rubbers is not expensive but it is time consuming to have to build a new one when you want to get on with the polishing itself. Also, you will waste polish if you leave a rubber lying about to go hard. Once a rubber hardens, throw it away; it will be of no further use.

For the first fad, simply slide the rubber on to the work and begin to move it back and forth in long strokes following the grain. Squeeze it between your fingers so that polish exudes on to the face of the rubber. And use a fair amount of pressure at this stage to force polish down into the open pores of the grain, but leave only a thin layer of polish on top of the work.

Some experts regard the fadding as finished once a sealing layer of polish covers the wood and the unevenness and crevices of the grain have been made flat. They then go on to the next process – 'bodying'. Others apply several fads, working each one into the grain until the surface is flat. For them, bodying is then a process of building up a thickness of polish.

For the home polisher, however, there is no real difference between fadding and bodying. Go on applying layers of polish with a rubber until the surface is flat.

Once you have applied the first coat and it has dried, you can apply successive coats with a variety of strokes. The basic action is a rhythmic movement in small circles, working along the surface and back, overlapping each line with the one before it [3.3]. Keep an even pressure on the rubber, any unevenness in the build-up of polish can be difficult and tedious to eliminate.

As a variation on the circular stroke, move the rubber in a figure-of-eight motion. The different stroke will help to avoid the build-up of polish in permanent circles [3.4].

The first fad is dry to the touch within about fifteen minutes of applying it, depending on the weather and the thickness of polish.

Before applying the second fad (or starting on the bodying process – whichever name you adopt) you must 'cut back' the polish.

Take a small sheet of extremely fine glasspaper or some 000 grade wire wool and gently rub down the surface.

This will remove the 'pips' or 'nibs', which are small particles of dirt stuck in the polish. More importantly, it will also remove the high spots of the polish itself, leaving a good thickness in the crevices of the grain and none over the peaks. If you take off the peaks between each application, the end result will be a completely flat layer of polish, with all the relief caused by the grain eliminated. That is the object of French polishing.

As you cut back the layer of polish, you will see pools of orange or light brown dust building up in the crevices. This dust is useful in showing how far you must go to achieve the flat surface you want. But remove the dust with a soft brush before applying the next layer of polish.

Once you are certain that you have a complete sealing layer over the wood, the process changes radically. From now on you will be using oil to aid the application of the polish. If there is the slightest crack in the early 'fad', the oil will seep down into the wood. This will not only produce dark stains, but will also prevent the polish adhering to the wood. Before long it will start to crack and peel off, and you will have to strip that area down and start again, and the oil will still affect the wood.

So, assuming the wood is completely sealed, take a bottle of white oil. (If you cannot obtain it, raw linseed oil will do.)

The oil serves two purposes. First it lubricates the already polished surface. Secondly it prevents the rubber lifting the polish already applied.

You will learn by experience how much to use. Professionals use a fair amount; home polishers would be wise to use as little as possible. The oil does not form part of the finish and must be removed at a later stage. Removing it is itself a skill and if carelessly done can ruin the work.

Professionals actually sprinkle oil on to the work and are quite happy to see a heavy smear as they apply the rubber of polish. This can be disconcerting to the beginner, so again it is wise to use as little oil as possible. Place your finger over the end of the bottle, tip it up, and slide your finger across the rim. You will be left with a smear of oil on your finger. Dab it on to the front of the rubber and it will lubricate the work just enough.

Now begin to work a new layer of polish on to the surface. Use the circular and figure-of-eight patterns and let your wrist do the work. If you have too much oil on the surface your rubber will slide over it. You will begin to grasp one of the essential elements in French polishing – 'pull'.

You may find yourself applying a good new layer of polish, but it will only lie on the surface and will build up eventually into a thick sticky coating. With 'pull', on the other hand, you can feel the new polish making contact with the surface of the old layer. The object is to blend the two together to form a cohesive coat. Too little pressure, and you will simply lay new layers of polish one on the other. Too much pressure, and the rubber will grab, so that you pull the old polish right off the surface and especially out of the grain pores. Then you will have to go back to the beginning.

You can only find the right pressure by experience. As a rough guide, it feels rather like pulling your hand across a pane of glass. If your hand has the normal amount of sweat on it, it will set up an action with the surface of the glass. If you wash your hand and dry it with powder, it will slide across the glass with no adhesion. If you let it get too sticky, you will set up a 'judder'. In French polishing, the ideal lies in the middle of this range. You can vary the amount of polish in the rubber and the pressure you apply to the work, and the amount of oil on the surface, and the amount of cutting back you do.

To summarise:

Fadding (a) you will have applied the first fad with a moderately wet rubber and some degree of pressure.

(b) you will have cut back the surface with glasspaper or wire wool, and brushed every trace of dust off the surface.

(c) you will have applied a second fad, and perhaps a third, to ensure that the wood is completely sealed with polish.

You will then have gone on with:

Bodying (d) applying a coat of polish with a variety of strokes, lubricating the job with a smear of oil.

(e) you will have cut it back, applied another coat, cut it back again, and applied another coat, until you have a flat and reasonably shiny surface. You must leave at least twenty-four hours after applying each coat before cutting it back and applying the next coat. You may find it still contains traces of the oil in the form of dull smears. You now come to the last stage in the process, called, appropriately:

Finishing There are several methods of finishing a coat of French polish. The easiest and most widely used is called 'spiriting off'.

Make up a new rubber and charge it sparingly with methylated spirits. With the face of the rubber nearly dry, work it over the surface of the work with a light stroke, starting with small circles and finishing with long straight strokes. The methylated spirits lifts off any oil that remains on the surface. At the same time the rubbing action re-works the fine top layer of the polish to burnish it into a bright fine finish.

The art of spiriting off is to judge how dry to make the rubber. Too wet, and the excess spirits will simply dissolve the polish, and you will have to go back to the bodying process to recover the flatness you need. Too dry, and it will leave a dull surface, with nothing achieved.

Some polishers simply invert a bottle of methylated spirits in their hand to leave a smear in the palm, and dip the polishing rubber into it, to pick up a surface layer of spirit. Lightly running this from end to end over the work will pick up the oil, and leave the work burnished to a good shine. Other polishers achieve a gradual change from polish to spirits by charging the rubber with methylated spirits in the later stages of the job. The spirits follows the polish through to the face of the rubber, and works the final body into a flat shining surface.

You can try these different methods on practice pieces to see which suits you before you start work on your best furniture.

The second method, known as 'stiffing', does not use methylated spirits, and is really an extension of the bodying process. It is useful where there are no oil smears to remove. You can use your ordinary bodying rubber or keep one specially for this operation. The key to success is to have the rubber almost dry. Charge it with polish very sparingly. Twist the neck firmly to force all excess polish out of the face, dab it away on to your tile or sheet of glass. As you relax the twisting action you will see that the polish seeps back into the rubber, leaving the surface almost dry.

Now, with a very light stroke, work the rubber in long straight lines from one end of the work to the other. This time the rubber itself will lift any smears of oil left in preceding stages and at the same time pull the polish into a good shine. As you work you will find that with no oil, and the rubber almost dry, the 'pull' will become more and more stiff; hence the name.

Various other methods have evolved during the 180 years since French polishing was introduced, all aimed at removing the oil and producing a final hard shine. They are fairly complicated and involve buying extra materials, many of which are no longer freely available.

Any enthusiast anxious to experiment with these obscure methods of polishing will enjoy researching the details in old craftsman's texts in a library.

4 Upholstery

A DROP-IN SEAT

The ideal place to start building up your skill as an upholsterer is with the same simple dining chair that gave you a start in the craft of restoration and repair. It should have a drop-in seat.

Push out the seat from underneath. On top it has a cover made of either fabric or hide. Turn it over. You will probably find a sheet of hessian or black lining tacked over the underside. Does it sag in the middle? A few years of sitting on it for two or three meals a day may well have taken the tension out of the support. Turn it back again. Does the top look as firm as it should? Or is there a pronounced dip that corresponds to the sagging on the underside? Is the fabric itself soiled from years of use and ready for replacement? Or would you simply welcome a change?

Ripping off

The first task in almost every upholstery operation is to strip the chair down to the bare frame.

For this operation you will need a ripping chisel and a mallet. A ripping chisel comes either straight or with a cranked blade; which you buy is a matter of preference. Or you can follow many upholsterers and use an old screwdriver. If the blade is badly worn, grind it down to give a well squared-off end. It should not be so sharp that it cuts through the tack and leaves a spike of metal in the wood.

Work on the underside first. Secure the seat either to your bench with a G-cramp or in a vice. Start near one corner, push the end of the chisel against the head of a tack, or under it if you possibly can, and hit the chisel firmly with the mallet. At the same time, drop your hand a couple of inches. This will have a levering effect on the tack, and it should flip out neatly. It may take two blows, the first to bend up the head of the tack, the second to force the tack out of the wood. Take care to knock in the direction of the grain, that is along the length of the seat frame, not across it. If you try the latter you may well split the wood or break the tack.

Work round the seat, removing the tacks that hold the lining in place. Now you will probably see how the top covering folds over to the underside of the seat, and how it is tacked down. Notice how, at the corner, the cover is pulled over, trimmed, and nailed down with an overlap. If you are just beginning upholstery, you would do well to make a rough sketch of the way the corner is formed.

Work round the piece again, knocking out all the tacks that hold the covering in place. This will expose either a layer of wadding – a white fluffy material like loose sheep's wool (if so lay this aside) – or a taut covering of white calico. If the latter, knock out any tacks holding it. You will then see the wadding underneath.

After removing the calico and wadding, you will come to the stuffing. The type you should look out for is horsehair. It has an indefinite life and in most craftsmen's opinion gives the best finish. Being rare, it is also extremely valuable. A professional upholsterer can get it carded (combed out free of tangles) to use again and may pay you a small sum for yours. Or you might be able to get it carded yourself and re-use it. If you can't get horsehair you will turn to one of the three forms of stuffing most widely available today – sea grass, coconut fibre or hog's hair. If foam rubber emerges from the chair, in any condition, reject it. No-one yet knows how long the life of foam rubber is in furniture.

Finally, in stripping down your chair, you will come to the upholstery support. This may be a set of springs, but in a seat of this type is more likely to be simple webbing. Go round the frame again, knocking out the tacks, until you have ripped off all the old webbing and are left with the bare frame. If there are flat springs screwed securely to the frame, leave them in place.

If you break the heads off any of the tacks, pull them out with pincers. Either that or knock them well in with a fine punch. You do not want any jagged edges to damage your new upholstery.

Before you start replacing the fabric, you must make sure that the frame is sound. While you must make the structure strong, you do not, of course, have to worry about appearance. The carpentry, which is not difficult, is described in Chapter 1.

Tack holes may look innocuous and will not be seen in the finished chair, but they can be a problem when hammering a line of new tacks in. Mix up a thick paste from sawdust and glue. Using a flexible blade, press the paste into the holes all over the chair. Use a damp cloth to wipe away the excess before it dries hard, and leave the chair for at least a day before you work on it again. You will find you have improved both the appearance and the structural soundness of the chair.

Replacing the webbing
Almost all upholstered chairs use webbing as a base, even if the seat also has springs. So fitting the webbing is the first task in re-upholstering.

You will need the following tools and materials, none of which are expensive:
Upholsterer's hammer A small hammer with a thin handle, available with a magnetic head for picking up tacks and holding them ready for hammering in. It works as an extra hand and is recommended. There are two types. One has a claw opposite to the hammer head for removing badly placed tacks. The other has a magnetic head for starting the tack and a solid head for knocking it home.
Upholsterer's nails These are blue metal tacks, available in various sizes. Upholsterers use 10mm, 13mm or 15mm according to the job they are doing. They also come in two versions: 'improved' tacks have large heads; 'fine' tacks have smaller heads. A box each of all six sizes will cover the full range of operations.
Webbing stretcher You can buy a tool made for the job, in one of two main designs. The correct tool is worth having for the control it gives. As an alternative you can use an offcut of wood, say a 100mm or 150mm length of 50mm × 40mm.
Webbing Buy the strongest available. Most upholsterer's stockists sell rolls of English webbing, which is perfect for any job. Jute webbing from the Far East is also available, but can only be used when perfectly dry.

Fixing the webbing

The illustrations [**4.1a–f**] show just how to attach the webbing. Mark the positions on the seat frame. If you are having an odd number of strips, start at the middle; otherwise start spacing them on each side of the centre. Work on the front-to-back webbing first; it is easier to get the first webbings properly spaced for equal balance on each side. Hold one end of the webbing over one of the frame members, leaving a 25mm overhang. Put in the first tack [**4.1a**] just outside the centre line of the wood. Put two more tacks just inside the centre line, to form the bottom points of a letter W. Now turn the overhang of webbing back over these tacks, and nail in two more on the line of the first one, to form the top outer points of the W. They should be close to the edges of the webbing. The pattern is shown in [**4.1b**], although the first three tacks will not of course now be visible.

The tacks are staggered, as five in a row might split the frame; they should lie comfortably over the centre line of the frame for strength.

Take care how you knock them in. Each one should be level with the surface. The sharp rim of the head of a bent tack will cut into the webbing and in time weaken the seat.

Now thread the webbing through the webbing stretcher and tighten it in the way shown in [**4.1c and d**].

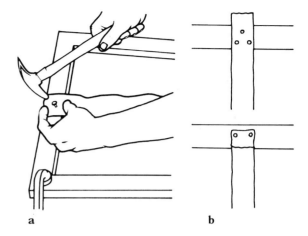

4.1a Tack home the free end of the webbing roll over the centre of one side of the frame.
b Locate the tacks in a 'W' to ensure strength without splitting.

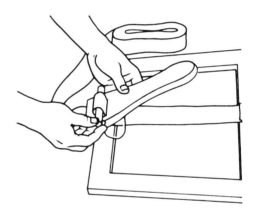

c Loop the webbing through the stretcher and insert the peg.

d Draw the stretcher over and adjust the webbing so that it will pull taut.

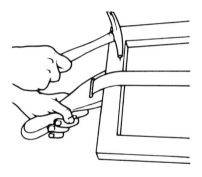

e Press down carefully on the stretcher and hammer home a 'W' pattern of tacks.

f Trim off the webbing with 25mm to spare for later over-turning.

Take up a tack on the end of your hammer and gently lever down the end of the stretcher [**4.1e**]. It will draw the webbing tight across the frame. Do not over-stretch or you will pull the webbing out of shape and weaken it. Aim to keep uniform tension across its width. This will give a firmer base for the stuffing.

If you have decided to economise and work with your home-made stretcher, wrap the webbing over the end of the block of wood. Grip the two tightly together, lever the block down against the side of the frame to pull the webbing taut, and hammer home the tacks.

Whichever system you use, hold the webbing in place with five tacks in the W pattern already shown. Some upholsterers knock in three tacks and add the other two later with the hessian. But it is vital to get the webbing under-tension right across its width, and this can only be done if the webbing stretcher is used for all five tacks. Knock in the outer two close to the edges and cut off the webbing leaving 25mm of overhang [**4.1f**].

Nail on the other strips of webbing, leaving about a 13mm gap between them. Smaller seats may take four strips, larger ones five. If the seat is wider at the front than at the back, fan the webbing out slightly to give even support.

Nail on the side-to-side webbing in exactly the same way, but thread the webbing through the first strips to give a woven effect before fixing it [**4.2**]. When finished, the webbing should be taut throughout.

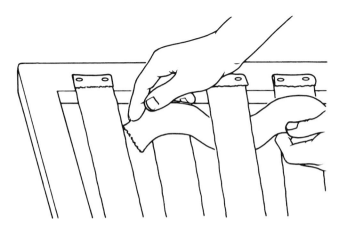

4.2 Thread the free end of the webbing roll through the fixed strands of webbing.

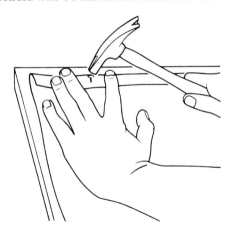

4.3a   Tack down a square of hessian to cover the webbing, with a 13mm over-turn.

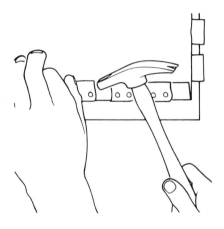

b   At the opposite side, tack down the webbing and hessian together.

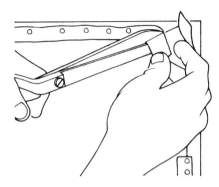

c   Trim the corners of the hessian to ensure that it lies flat.

The hessian cover

Lay the frame on a piece of upholsterer's hessian and cut it tidily to fit round the outer edge with an overhang of about 13mm.

With the upholsterer's hammer and some tacks, tack it down one side – 10mm improved are right for this job, as the hessian is not meant to take strain, only to stop the stuffing falling through the webbing.

You can either fold the hessian over first, and tack it down through the double layer, or you can tack down one layer, then fold it over, rather as you folded the webbing itself, and tack down the fold with the second row of tacks alternating with the first, and only the second row showing [**4.3a**].

Now pull the hessian taut across the frame. You will have to do this by hand, pulling it at the point you are tacking, unless you have another simple tool, a hide stretcher. This is a pair of pincers with long square jaws which grip about 75mm of material so that you can pull it taut by a levering action. They make the job much easier. The reason for tacking half under and half over the fold should now be obvious. You can get much firmer tension on the hessian if you pull it from the edge and tack through the single thickness. On two of the sides you will have an end of webbing hanging loose. Turn this over along with the fold of hessian, and tack the two down together [**4.3b**].

The tacks in the hessian should be at about 200mm intervals, *outside* the rows of tacks holding the webbing. This gives a tidy finish and avoids the risk of splitting the wood.

A complication arises at the corners, where you will find yourself with a fold of excess hessian, this could stop the seat frame sitting comfortably on the corner blocks.

It is better to trim off the hessian at the corner. Either snip off the diagonal, then fold the two corners over to form a mitre, or cut out the corner square and turn one fold over the other [**4.3c**]. Either method will give a tidy finish.

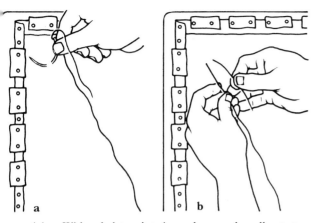

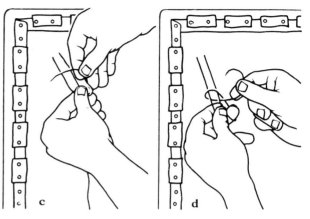

4.4a With upholsterer's twine and a curved needle, start sewing a pattern of bridles.
b Secure the twine with a slip knot. First draw it through to within 10cm inches of the end.

c Turn the short end over both parts of the twine to form a letter 'D'.
d Pass the end of the twine up through the open loop of the 'D'.

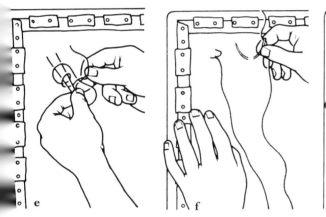

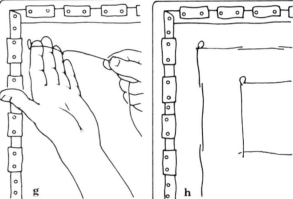

e Pass the short end over again and up through the 'D' for a second time. Draw the knot tight.
f Sew a stitch along, back, and up through the hessian to form the first bridle.

g Draw the bridle tight enough to accommodate three fingers flat against the hessian.
h A well-balanced pattern of bridles will hold the stuffing in place all over the seat.

Bridles

The next step is to put in some 'bridles' (or 'stuffing ties') – loops of twine that will hold the stuffing firmly in place. You will need a curved needle and some upholsterer's thread. If the thread is too thick for the eye of the needle, hammer the end flat or use a larger needle.

First, secure the end of the twine. Push the needle into the hessian about 60mm diagonally in from one corner of the frame and back up through it, picking up about three strands of the hessian. Pull the thread through to within 100mm of the end. Now tie an upholsterer's slip knot; [**4.4a–e**] shows the technique.

Now start making bridles along one side of the frame. Form a big looping stitch about 75mm long, push the needle down through the hessian and back up a few strands away in the direction you came from. Pull the stitch just taut enough to allow you to get three fingers under the thread [**4.4f–g**].

Continue the bridles along the side of the frame, turn, and go along the other sides. Then put some in the centre of this square. Either cross the diagonal, though this could cause an imbalance in the stuffing in time, or form a second small square. An alternative is to stitch the bridles in parallel lines.

Stuffing

Upholstery stuffing comes in plastic bags, and at first you will have to take your supplier's advice on how much you need, but will soon be able to judge fairly accurately how much chairs of various sizes take.

There are, as mentioned earlier, three main kinds: sea grass, coconut fibre and hog's hair. Horsehair is unreasonably expensive The best policy is to use the highest quality stuffing material you can afford, preferably hog's hair.

Pull a handful of stuffing off your supply, tease it out neatly and tuck it under the first bridle. Make it fairly firm, but not enough to pull the slack out of the other bridles. Go on tucking handfuls under all the bridles until you have a pattern of stuffing held firmly in place, so that the whole finished upholstery does not drift off to one side and throw the seat out of shape when in use.

Next, lay more stuffing in between the rows you have tied down, and then on top, until you have a good dome shape. You will have to develop your judgement as your experience grows. In the first instance, it is advisable to err on the generous side, as the stuffing will be compressed down in use. A pile 125mm–150mm high is not too much to produce stuffing 50mm thick when the seat is finished.

Calico covering

Cut off a square of calico big enough to cover the stuffing and overlap the side of the frame by 50mm. Lay it over the stuffing. Taking care not to pull the stuffing out of place, knock in a tack (halfway only) along one outer edge of the frame. Turn round the frame, ease the calico taut, and knock in a tack halfway along the opposite edge [**4.5a**]. Then put a tack in each of the other two edges; now you can handle the seat without the stuffing falling out.

Lay out a few tacks and your hammer on the workbench. The right tacks for this job are 'fine' tacks. Calico is a fine-weave material, so their small unobtrusive heads are adequate. A suitable length is 10mm.

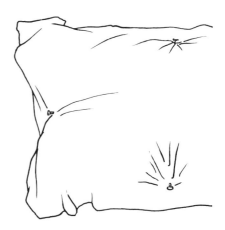

4.5a   Cover the hair with wadding, then tear a square of calico and secure it initially with a single temporary tack on each edge.

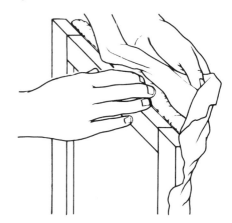

b   Stand the frame on an edge and begin smoothing out the calico. Tuck in the wadding so that it does not overhang the frame.

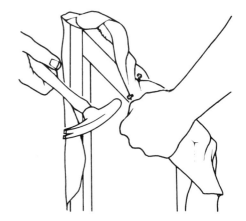

c   Hammer in a temporary tack to secure the calico on the underside of the frame. A line of three, centrally placed, will secure one side while you work on the other three sides.

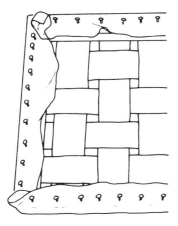

d Work towards the corners, until you have the calico well smoothed out and secure.

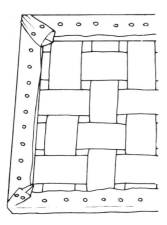

e Draw the calico up into a neat fold at the corners. Trim off any excess. Tack it down at each side of the fold for a firm, neat, flat finish.

Turn the seat on to one edge. Holding the calico in place, remove the tack on the upper edge. Now take the end of the calico in one hand, and start to ease it taut across the top of the stuffing with the other. Do not pull the calico; you will only stretch it out of shape. Instead, keep holding the calico steady with one hand and compress the stuffing, drawing your hand firmly across it with the other. As you compress it the tension will ease, the calico will slacken, and you can simply

take up the slack. Do not pull too hard at this stage; there is still the opposite side to work on. Tuck the stuffing back into the seat as you go. Avoid leaving any hair hanging over the edge; it may leave ugly marks and could make the chair frame too wide to fit back into the chair. When you are satisfied you have eased the calico to a fair tension, nail it down temporarily, with a tack knocked half way in, on the underside of the frame. Add another temporary tack 25mm along towards one corner, and a third 25mm along towards the other corner.

Turn the frame round and do exactly the same job on the opposite side, finishing with three temporary tacks. These tacks should be in line about 25mm in from the outer edge of the frame. Turn the frame round again and complete the other two sides [**4.5b,c**].

Now add the remaining tacks, 25mm apart all around. Work from one set of three, towards the corner away from you, then towards the corner nearest to you. Compress the stuffing, ease your hand over it, tuck in the hair, take up the slack, and knock in a tack. Keep up this operation coaxing the material into a smooth curve, until you get close to the corners. You will then be left with a fold of material at each corner [**4.5d**].

It would be easy if you could cut away all the excess material but this would leave raw edges which could either fray or pull away leaving the stuffing inadequately covered. The problem could also be solved by turning the material under but this would produce too much bulk.

The answer lies in a compromise. First stretch the calico over the corner, pulling it towards the centre of the seat frame, and tack it down. Now cut away all the excess, level with the inner edge of the frame. You will now have two small folds, one on either side of the first tack. Pull the first fold up, roll the material under itself towards the first tack, and lay the fold neatly down towards the outer edge of the frame. Tack it down. Do the same on the second fold. Trim off the excess material. This operation is among the most difficult to do well, as calico stretches easily. Fortunately the final result does not need to be too neat, as it will be invisible on the finished chair [**4.5e**].

Finally, knock home all the temporary tacks and trim off the calico to a neat line all round the frame.

Wadding

The drawback to upholstery stuffing is that prickly ends of hair find their way through the weave of calico. Wadding, which forms a barrier which the hairs or fibres cannot penetrate, cures the problem. One layer of wadding should be enough; some upholsterers prefer two.

Some upholsterers also prefer to put the wadding next to the stuffing, under the calico. Both methods are perfectly acceptable.

Tear the wadding to fit exactly to the outer top edge of the frame and lay it in place. A similar material called linter's felt is also used for this job.

The covering

The final covering is fitted in much the same way as the calico. Make sure it goes on straight: if it is plain material get the weave dead square, or the seat will never look right; if there is a pattern, make sure it is both square and central. The great advantage of the first tack on each outer edge of the frame is that you can hammer it in while the frame is flat on the workbench, making sure that the material does not move out of true as you go.

With the material secured, turn the seat on to its edge, knock in the three temporary tacks, all round, then work to the corners. Check that the material is still square, since you may have eased it out of place as you took up the slack. If so, take out a few tacks and ease it back to the other side.

The corners are different from the calico corners. If you have a very stretchy material, you can take up any folds by pulling the material over the corner and securing it with a central tack. This time, fold the excess under itself towards the outer edge of the frame, and turn the material back down to form a mitre. Tack the first fold. Turn the second fold under and tack it down. On the front corners of the seat these two folds tend to overlap because of the slightly acute angles. Try to pull them towards the centre of the frame to form a flat mitre. If you cannot, simply tack them down and go on to the next corner.

You may find that the material has rucked slightly along the outer edges of the frame: this is almost inevitable with this technique and will not show once the seat is dropped into place in the chair.

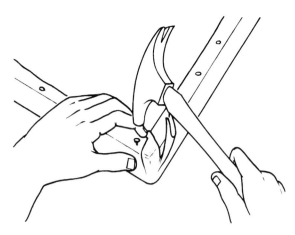

4.6 The top cover is fitted by the same method as the calico except at the corners. Draw the central part in and tack it down. Draw the sides in to form a double pleat. Trim off the excess.

If you have a material which does not lend itself to stretching, you can adopt a folding technique, although this might not work well on very thick coverings. First fold the material down the side edge of the frame. Then fold the front edge under itself at an angle of 45 degrees. The crease thus formed will lie neatly down the corner of the frame. On a drop-in-seat, you can leave the crease open, but it looks much neater if you sew it down using a slip stitch. This will also be good practice for the time when you have to sew this type of pleat on bigger chairs, and any faults in your first efforts will hardly show.

Now turn the trailing edges under the seat frame. There will be at least four layers. As you have sewn the material, you can cut away the excess carefully up to the sewn edge, and fold

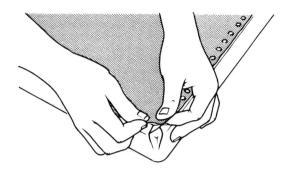

4.7 Add a dust cover of black lining, folded square at the corners.

down the spare as you did in the other method to form a neat mitre. Tack it in place [**4.6**].

Some upholsterers like to leave a drop-in seat finished in that condition, so that they can see any faults developing from the underside. A neater finish is achieved by adding a dust cover, for which a special black lining is available. Cut the black lining about 6mm bigger than the frame all around. Turn it back under by about 13mm, so that it lies 6mm inside the frame. Tack it all round with 6mm tacks, set 25mm apart. The corners are easy. Simply fold the material square, and square again, and tack it down. This material lies quite flat, so there is no need to worry about forming mitres or trimming away bulk [**4.7**]. The job is now finished.

A STUFFED-OVER SEAT

This type of seat represents a major step forward in upholstering technique, but still involves the experience gained from working on the drop-in seat. It is the kind in which the upholstery not only covers the top of the seat, but also reaches down the sides. It may be part of a dining suite, an occasional chair, or perhaps a desk chair. Make the frame structurally sound, fill in old tack holes with glue and sawdust, and chisel a 6mm bevel all round the outer edge of the frame.

Because there are no springs in this seat, the webbing must be fixed to the top edges of the frame. Follow the same procedure as for the drop-in seat. Remember that an extra strand of webbing is not expensive and it is not worth risking collapse by laying too few strips too far apart.

Attach the hessian, fitting it either with the same tacks as the webbing, or with an extra row of tacks outside the line of the end of the webbing. Hessian prevents the stuffing falling through the gaps in the webbing, so you must cut it snugly up to the corners. In [**4.8**] you will see that the tops of the front legs stand higher than the edge of the frame. You need to fit the hessian neatly into that corner, either with a mitre, or with a square cut, folding in the excess neatly.

Now go round the seat putting in the bridles. Start 75mm in from a corner and work along following each edge in turn and then fill in the centre. The pattern is not important, but sew the stitches symmetrically so that the finished seat will not, in time, become lopsided. Do not place bridles closer than 75mm from the edges of the frame. Later, you will be 'regulating' the stuffing – moving it about inside the partly covered seat by poking through the cover with a sharp tool – if the ties are too close to the frame this operation will be impossible.

First stuffing

In most chairs except the simple drop-in seat, stuffing is installed in two stages. The first, held firmly in place under a covering of hessian, forms a solid base for the upholstery. The second gives the seat its final shape.

When you have a satisfactory arrangement of bridles, start inserting the first stuffing. Tease out the hair to a uniform thickness and fit it neatly under the bridles with enough tension under each one to hold the stuffing in place. Then push more stuffing down between the lines to produce a roughly square area of stuffing covering the centre of the seat.

Next pack out the stuffing to the edges of the frame.

Start taking palm-sized chunks of stuffing, tease them out to an even consistency and tuck them in under the bridles that run round the outer edge of your square. Work with lumps of stuffing about 100mm long. Tuck them under the bridle so they reach towards the chair frame and overhang it slightly. Work round the seat keeping the stuffing well balanced. Push each additional lump under its predecessor, until the outer edge has built up to a fat springy lip round the frame [**4.8**].

Keep pressing it with your hand, first to ensure that it feels the same all round, secondly to estimate the thickness it will make when it is compacted later in the upholstering process.

Most chairs take more stuffing material than the inexperienced upholsterer would expect. The aim is to utilise two-thirds of the hair in the first stuffing, and one-third in the second.

When you have formed a substantial lip, and it holds well away from the frame under compression, cover it with 'scrim', the popular name for an open-weave hessian. The open weave allows flexibility; but it can also take up shapes you do not intend.

First cut a piece big enough to cover the seat and hang down the sides to the bottom of the frame. Cut it square to the weave; the lines of thread are important guides in keeping the upholstery even.

To make a square cut in scrim, hessian, or calico, first 'draw' a thread. Nick the selvedge with scissors and pull out one thread. It will leave a line for cutting which is square to the weave of the fabric.

Lay the scrim smoothly over the seat and ensure that the weave runs squarely front to back and side to side. Tack it with three temporary tacks into the sides of the frame, to hold the lip of stuffing in place [**4.9**].

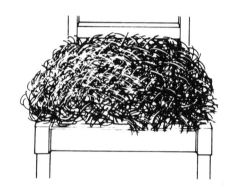

4.8   On a stuffed-over seat, apply webbing, hessian, bridles and a layer of stuffing as before. Tuck hair under the outer bridles to give a generous roll all round the frame.

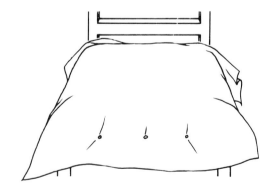

4.9   Cover the hair with a square of scrim, temporarily tacked down at the sides.

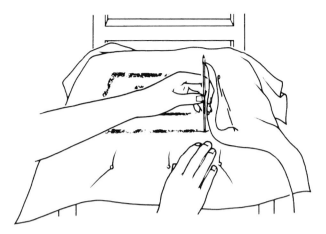

4.10 Sew a pattern of through-stuffing ties over the central part of the seat.

The next job is to put in 'through-stuffing' ties of upholstery thread to anchor the central body of the stuffing, and the scrim over it, to the base of the seat. Use a double-ended needle, a long instrument, sharp at both ends, with the eye at one end only. It is designed to go through thick layers of stuffing, hessian, webbing and any covering material, and then back, without having to be turned. It is easy to forget that the end from which you are pushing is as sharp as the leading end so be careful how you use it.

Double-ended needles are available in a range of sizes. A medium size (20cm) will be suitable for this job. Thread it with about a metre-and-a-half of medium twine.

Take a piece of chalk and draw a line on the scrim, 10cm in from the frame all round. Complete symmetry is important in all upholstery operations, so it is worth taking care with marking the shape.

At one corner of your square, push the needle down through the scrim, hair, hessian and webbing. Pull the twine through to within 15cm of the end. Now push the needle back up through the layers, about 8mm away from the downward thread, and pull it out at the top of the seat. Tie an upholsterer's slip knot in the end (see page 63), and draw it up tight.

Now make the first stitch, along one side of the square. Follow the principle used in tying bridles. Divide the length of the line into a convenient number of stitches, say three or four on the average drawing-room chair, and make each stitch this length. Push the needle down through the stuffing, out at the bottom, and back up about 8mm in the direction you came from. Then go on to the next stitch. The stitches will then loop over each other to give the strength and 'hold' you are looking for. Make a similar overlap at the corners and continue round the 'square' [**4.10**].

How you deal with the centre of the square depends largely on the size of the seat centre. On a small seat you can simply turn towards the centre, add one stitch, and finish in the centre of the seat. On a larger seat you can stitch in a separate little square of through-stuffing ties. However you do it, pull the ties tight as you go, then finally check them, pulling them tight again all round, and knot off the last stitch with several half-hitches.

You will now have a firm pad in the centre of the seat, forming a shallow depression as shown in [**4.10**].

Lay your double-ended needle carefully back in your tool box, with a cork on each end to prevent accidents.

69

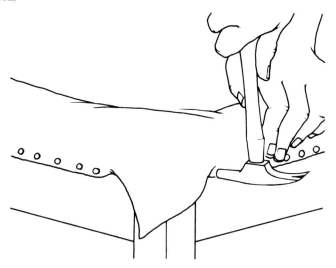

4.11a   Fold the scrim under, and tack it to the bevelled edge of the frame to produce a bulbous roll all round.

Preparing to sew a hard edge

For this you will need the upholsterer's hammer and a supply of the 10mm improved tacks.

Remove the temporary tacks from one side of the hessian. Draw it over the edge roll of hair and check that you have the right amount of hair in place. As you work on your second and subsequent chairs, you will have a better idea how far a given quantity of stuffing will reduce under compression, but on your first chair you will have to try to visualise what the finished seat will look like when all the stuffing round the frame has been tightly compressed. You must have enough hair in there to still overhang the edge, and rise to a point just below the final height of the centre of the chair seat when the job is complete.

You must also work out the right tension for the hessian round the edge roll: unfortunately, this is almost impossible to judge until you have worked through the next stage of the operation, and stitched the hard edge itself. Only then will you know how tightly the stitching will draw the edge; another case where you later efforts should show improvement over your first. For your first job draw the hessian taut over the stuffing, then let it out by about 6mm. The stitching in the hard edge will take up the slack.

When you have worked out the tension, try to estimate once more whether you have enough stuffing under it. If it looks too mean add more

now, before you have nailed down the scrim (this is the best time although you can do it later from the ends).

Next cut the scrim accurately about 25mm below the top of the frame. Remember that the stuffed-over seat has a bevelled edge on the outer top side of the frame. Fold the scrim under the stuffing and knock in tacks, about 25mm apart, through the double layer, into the bevelled edge. At this stage knock them only half-way home, allowing for future alterations.

You will now appreciate the value of keeping the scrim square. On the front and back edges of the chair seat, you can follow a line of the thread to ensure absolute symmetry, and you will soon see whether your stuffing is packed into the chair evenly at each side by the amount of slack the scrim shows. If the chair has an unsquare frame, you will not be able to follow a single line of thread. But you can judge, from the pattern of tacks crossing the weave, whether you are following a consistent line or whether your stuffing is out of balance.

Go round all four sides, folding under and temporarily tacking down the scrim on to the bevelled edge. Leave the corners open for the moment, see [**4.11a**].

The lip you have now formed should also be straight when viewed at eye level from the sides and front. If the roll is not level, now is the time to

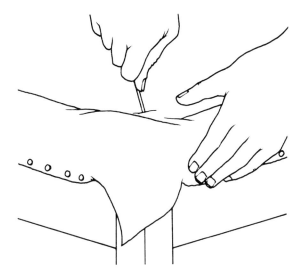

b Regulate the stuffing well forward, and well down on to the frame.

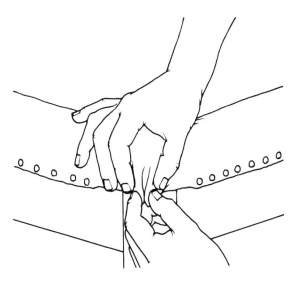

c After inserting any extra stuffing from the corners, close the ends with a pleat, tacked down and sewn.

correct it. The four sides are open at each end. If any part needs more stuffing, take handfuls, tease out the amount, push it in at the ends and move along.

Use a 'regulator' for this operation, a long strong spike with a sharp point at one end. Stab it through the scrim into the stuffing and adjust the levels of stuffing with it [**4.11b**].

When everything looks even and well shaped, hammer your tacks finally into the bevelled edge.

Only the four corners now remain. The rear corners, where the scrim meets the back uprights of the chair, are the easiest to deal with. Using scissors, carefully cut into the corner at a 45-degree angle. Stop just short of the chair back. Turn each side of the cut under and fold it away beneath the scrim as you go. Trim off the excess, fold it under itself along the bevelled edge with the remainder of the scrim, and tack it down. Do this at both rear posts.

The method of treating the front corners will vary with the design of chair. In this case simply cut and turn the scrim under to follow the outline of the legs, and nail in a tack halfway along each to hold the scrim in place. A large flap of excess material will remain. Pull this taut and check that you have enough stuffing in the corners.

Stitching the hard edge will draw the front corners back towards the centre of the seat, so you must have plenty of stuffing there. The corner should overhang the frame, viewed from both the front and the side. If there is not enough, push in some more stuffing under the corners and work into place with the regulator.

Now turn the flap inside out and tuck in the excess material so that the fold is formed inside the chair. You will have two folded edges that come together [**4.11c**]. Thread a curved needle with fine upholstery twine and sew these edges together. You may have practiced this piece of sewing on the calico of your drop-in seat. If not, it is a simple ladder or slip stitch, as shown on page 109.

When you have sewn far enough down, fold the scrim under, and put a tack through the folds to hold it on the exact corner of the seat frame. Trim any excess. Hammer home the temporary tacks all round.

You will now have a bulbous border, filled like a sausage, covered rather loosely with scrim and firmly tacked in place ready for the next stage.

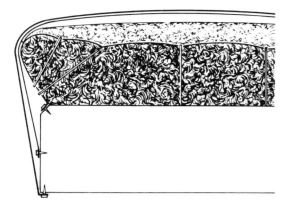

4.12a Section showing the composition of a hard edge on a stuffed-over seat.

Sewing a hard edge

A hard edge all round a seat is important. It gives comfort and support to the sitter and keeps the upholstery firmly in place. The hard edge is in the form of a compact roll, made by moving the stuffing into position, then securing it by sewing lines of stitches through it with upholstery twine.

It is not possible to produce a totally even filling during the stuffing process itself, nor to lay the scrim perfectly over the stuffing. You can only achieve a perfect roll *after* the scrim is in place. The regulator therefore serves not only to correct mistakes made earlier, but also to move the stuffing into exactly the position required.

Again, stab the regulator into the top of the thick 'sausage' of stuffing you have formed. With a circular action, lever the handle away from you so that the pointed end draws the stuffing towards you.

Do not 'pick' but make bold movements of large wads of stuffing. Move the stuffing to one side or the other to eliminate any unevenness. But most important, pull it forward to fill out the roll of scrim directly above the edges of the seat frame.

The outer curve of the stuffing should overhang the edge of the frame by about 6mm to 13mm. Then, when the calico and top cover are later applied, they will lie clear of the edge of the wood. See [**4.12a**].

When you have drawn the stuffing well forward, push in the regulator from the front and, with the same circular motion, pull the stuffing down to pack it on to the top of the frame edge. Fill this space with a compact layer of stuffing. Remember that this edge will take much pressure in use and that it must hold steady. A firm full edge, right to the front and bottom of the roll, is essential.

If you do not have enough stuffing in the roll, open up one end and add more, working the whole mass along from the ends with the regulator. Work all round the edge of the chair – front, sides and back – to produce a straight line. You may have some difficulty using the regulator on the rear edge because the chair back itself will present an obstruction. Fortunately, this matters least because the rear edge will not take any direct weight.

At first you can try to get all the edges level. But with experience you will be able to graduate the side downwards from front to back, to give a more elegant 'set' to the chair seat. Regulate the front and back first, to give the right respective heights, then regulate the sides in turn between them.

When satisfied that you have a full roll all round with a straight top edge, well compacted on to the frame itself, and overhanging slightly, lay aside the regulator.

Next, stitch the stuffing into a firm roll all round to produce the hard edge. Two types of stitch are used: 'blind stitch', and 'top stitch'. At this stage you may need a pair of good strong leather gloves to stop the twine cutting into your fingers.

Blind stitch

Take up the double-pointed needle (the 20cm model will do for this edge) and thread it with about a metre of upholsterer's medium twine. Turn the back of the chair towards you. Begin where you can correct your mistakes before coming to the more visible sides and front.

First fix the twine with a single stitch. Almost all upholstery stitching is done from left to right, so start 13mm in from the left-hand corner and close to the wood of the frame. Push the needle in through the stuffing, at an angle of about 30 degrees above the horizontal, so that the point

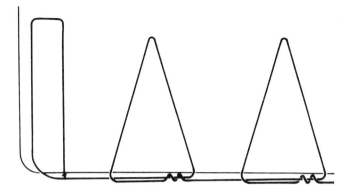

b   Plan of the path of blind stitches through a hard edge.

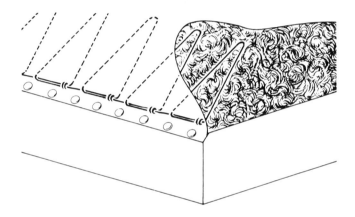

c   The stitches do not come through the scrim.

emerges about 75mm in from the edge of the frame. Pull it right through. Now go back towards your left, 13mm, and push the needle back through the stuffing so that it emerges right down in the corner, 13mm back from the point where you started. Pull the twine through and tie it in an upholsterer's slip knot. This will give you a firm starting stitch [**4.12b**].

Begin your first row, consisting of blind stitches, so called because the twine does not come right through the upholstery.

Estimate about 40mm along from the knot you have just made. Measure the first stitch if you wish. But you will soon be able to judge the correct distance and produce a row of equally spaced stitches. Push in the needle, again close to the wooden frame, and at the same 30-degree angle as the first stitch. Instead of pushing it straight in at right angles to the chair frame, angle it backwards

slightly to your left, so that the point emerges approximately 13mm back along the line.

Pull the needle with one hand and push it with the other, but not right through. Ease it forward until the eye just begins to show through the scrim. Now re-angle the needle, turning the point towards the right so that the eye end points towards the left. Push it back, the threaded end leading, through the stuffing. You will see now why a double-pointed needle is essential. Keep it at a constant angle so that it emerges just above the edge of the frame, and 25mm along from the point where it went in. The twine will now have followed an angled path through the stuffing without emerging from the scrim [**4.12c**].

When you pull that stitch tight, it will pick up a wedge of stuffing and draw it into a compact mass.

4.13   Locking the stitches in a hard edge is the same technique for blind and top stitches. Return the needle by its sharp rear end, loop the twine twice around it, then withdraw the needle and take it away to the right. Give a tug on the twine to pull the stitch to a firm locked loop.

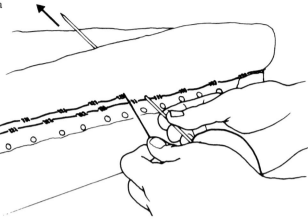

To form the stitch itself, draw the needle out of the stuffing towards you for about 50mm. Take up the twine in your left hand, about 15mm from the eye of the needle. Make two turns in this twine round the protruding end of the needle in an anti-clockwise direction. Now pull the needle the rest of the way through those loops and out of the stuffing. You have produced what looks like a tangle of twine, but the reason will soon become clear.

Pull the needle away to your right and jab it firmly into the upholstery well out of the way on the right-hand side of the chair. Next, pull it through the stuffing to take up the slack, and finally tug it firmly to the right. Two things will happen. The twine passing through the roll will draw the stuffing into a compact hard edge, and the 'tangle' will snap into a neat rolled stitch, resembling a piece of twirled candy. The twists produced with that double looping motion will prevent the stitch working loose. Each stitch will then take the strain individually and even if one stitch should break in later years, the remainder will stay firm [**4.13**].

Continue, moving 40mm along to the right for each stitch, inserting the needle at an angle back towards the left, pulling it through until the eye shows, pushing it back through at an angle to the left so that it emerges 25mm back from the point where it went in. Twist two loops round the needle, anti-clockwise. Pull the needle through, secure it safely out of the way, and pull the stitch tight. Repeat along the row.

As you proceed you will form a compact roll. Try to keep it even. The stitches should be at the same intervals and the roll itself free of bulges. If uneven patches appear, use your regulator to pull more stuffing into weak areas, or take it away from over-stuffed parts.

Follow the corners round as accurately as possible. On the last stitch of an edge, instead of working back to your left, turn the needle the other way, and push it back to emerge right down in the bottom left corner of the next edge.

To join fresh lengths of twine, cut off your next convenient length and simply tie a reef knot in it as close to the scrim as possible. The knot should fall between two stitches with no superfluous loop.

When you reach the end of the final edge, pull the last stitch tight and secure it with a couple of knots stitched in with the needle.

In some seats, the hard edge will be so fat that a second row of blind stitches is required, about 13mm above the first. This generally applies to thickly padded armchairs. In the case of a stuffed-over seat, one row of blind stitches will probably be enough, and you can proceed to top stitching.

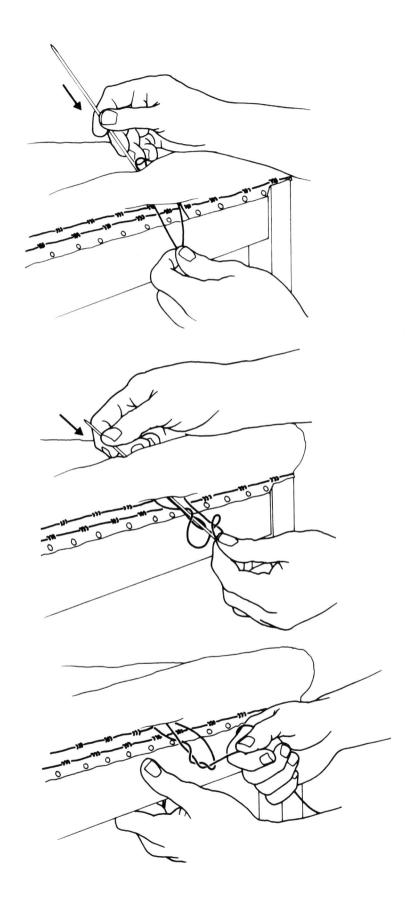

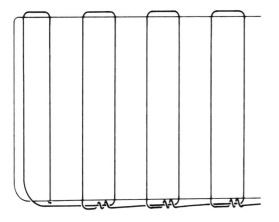

4.14a Top stitches through a hard edge.

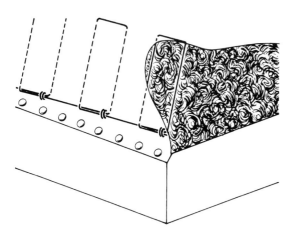

b Section shows path of top stitches.

Top stitch

Top stitching is similar to blind stitching in many respects. Start the row similarly, at the left-hand end, with a slip knot. This row of stitches should be approximately 6mm above the row of blind stitches. This time, move just 25mm to the right to begin each stitch, and push the needle directly through the stuffing. Do not angle it to the side. Make sure it follows the same angle to the horizontal as the blind stitches. The needle should emerge about 13mm nearer to the frame. Pull it right through and out on the other side of the scrim. For this type of stitch, as you have pulled the needle through, you can obviously turn it round and use the non-threaded point. Move back 13mm along the row and return the needle

back through the stuffing towards you, parallel with the ingoing twine. It will emerge 13mm to the left. Loop the twine twice round the needle exactly as before. Pull the needle through, stick it into the upholstery, well to the right out of harm's way, and pull the stitches tight with a good final tug to the right [**4.14**].

At this stage, examine carefully the roll you are making. This is the last stage at which you can determine the shape of the hard edge. As you draw the top stitching tight, the edge should be firm, well stuffed, well secured and absolutely even all the way along. It should be dead straight along the front and back, perhaps sloping slightly down towards the back of the seat on the side edges.

Several faults may appear. The stuffing still may not be evenly distributed. Correct that with the regulator. The roll may fall like a lip over the edge of the frame, when you press it with a hand. Correct this tendency by stitching the top row on a lower slant, so that the needle emerges closer to the centre of the chair seat, and thereby pulling the roll back. The roll may sit on the top of the frame, without the necessary overhang. Correct this fault by inserting your needle nearer to the vertical. Pulling the stitches tight will then move the roll towards the edge of the frame. Finally, the roll itself may be weak and insufficiently padded. There is no way to insert more stuffing at this stage. The best plan is to go along the weak edges and insert another row of top stitching an equal distance above the first. The extra stitches will pull the roll right. Of course, having to do this means that you should have catered for the problem earlier with that extra row of blind stitches. But only experience will show you how to decide how many rows you need.

Work right round the seat as you did on the blind stitched row, and knot off the twine as before. You have now completed the hard edge.

The technique of sewing a hard edge is among the most widely employed skills in upholstery. They appear in stuffed–over seats, along the front of large upholstered pieces, round the wings of wing-chairs, on chair arms of almost all types, and round many padded backs.

The size of the hard edge varies considerably from one chair to another but the process remains the same.

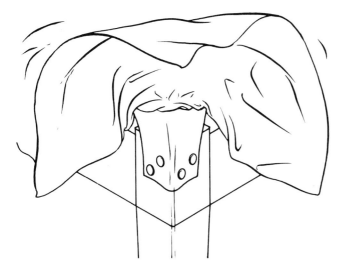

4.15   Card tacked in place to form a neat corner.

Second stuffing

The chair seat is in the form of a dish, with a firm edge slightly overhanging the frame all round. Now you can add the second stuffing.

Start by sewing in a few more bridles, using your curved needle to loop the twine through the scrim and back on itself.

A run of bridles between the through-stuffing ties and the hard edge may be enough. But test the through-stuffing ties themselves. If you can lift them slightly, use them to secure the second stuffing. If they are too tight, sew in another set of bridles among the through-stuffing ties.

Add the final third of your stuffing. Tuck it under all the bridles, then fill in the gaps. Fill the space between the outer bridles and the hard edge particularly well, especially just behind the front edge.

Tear a layer of felt or wadding, big enough to cover the curved dome of stuffing and to reach well on to the hard edge. This is to prevent the hair coming through, so take care not to tear it off too short. Lay it in place.

Cut a calico covering fairly generously, and begin fixing it with two or three temporary tacks on each side, about one-third of the distance down the side of the frame. (Like the procedure for the drop-in seat.) Of course, you cannot turn the complete chair in your hands conveniently, but you can still press down on the top of the seat to take up the slack. Work steadily round the frame, using temporary tacking at first. You may find the calico has a tendency to distort as you smooth out the slack and tack it down. At any point where this occurs, take out the tacks and keep working the material against the direction of distortion to get it as straight as you possibly can. Tack from the centre of each side to within about two inches of the corners. Use the weave of the calico as a guide to keep the covering square.

Cut a small square out of light card. Fold it in half, and wrap it round the corner of the stuffing between the underlip of the hard edge and the top of the frame, see [**4.15**]. Tack it in place, tucking a small lump of wadding behind it. This will help give a firm appearance to the chair once it is covered.

77

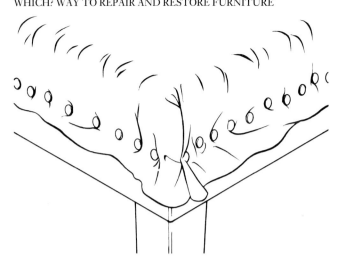

4.16 Calico tacked in place.

Now complete the calico corners. First the back. Cut into the corner again, diagonally until you meet the inside back of the chair. Fold each side of the cut away under the calico, and again trim off the excess. You will find a new use for the regulator here. Turn it round and use the flattened end to tuck the material neatly into the corner where it meets the chair leg. You can hold the material taut with one hand and fold and tuck the calico with the flat end of the regulator. You will achieve a far better finish this way. Finally tack it in place.

At the front, carefully draw the calico taut over the corner and push the fold from the front round the side. Then pull the side calico down over that first fold. You will be left with a pocket, visible from the front but not from the side. Tidy up the fold with the flat end of your regulator, remaking the fold as many times as necessary to get a neat pleat from the crown of the corner directly down the angle. Then tack the calico in place. Finally sew up the open end of the pocket using an ordinary slip stitch [4.16].

The chair is now ready for its final covering. If the fabric has a pattern, you should have sufficient to fit the design symmetrically, either centrally if it is a large motif, or evenly balanced on both sides of the chair if it is a smaller one.

Measure the chair with a flexible linen tape measure in both directions, over the calico, down the faces of the frame, and underneath the edges of the frame, to calculate the amount of fabric required.

Fitting the covering material is relatively easy. You have done most of the hard work at the calico stage. For extra comfort, and to stop any stray hairs from the stuffing coming up through the cover, it is worth fitting a new layer of thin wadding on the chair. Lay it in place, running it down the sides of the frame and under the edge, so that it will soften all the wooden corners. If it is not wide enough to cover the whole chair, lay it in parts, separating the layers where the edges of the wadding meet, and relaying them interleaved, as though pushing together two halves of a pack of playing cards.

Now apply the top cover, making sure you lay it on straight and that the pattern is well balanced. If there is a definite direction to the design, the top is at the back of the chair and the bottom at the front. Fixing is almost the same as with the calico cover. Temporarily tack it on the centre of each side, on the underside of the frame, then cut diagonally into the back uprights. Tuck it away with the flat regulator end and continue the tacking to the corners.

At the front, you may follow the procedure for the calico by leaving a single exposed pleat. Generally speaking, it makes sense to sew it using a suitable matching thread. Otherwise the pleat tends to gape eventually and look unsightly.

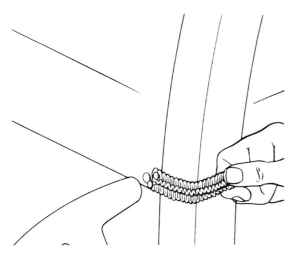

4.17a Fixing braid. Tack end.

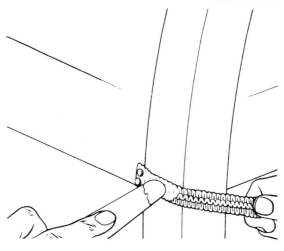

b Apply adhesive.

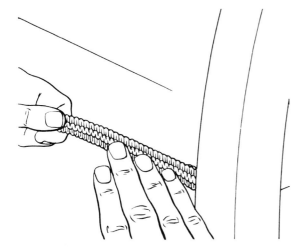

c Smooth down.

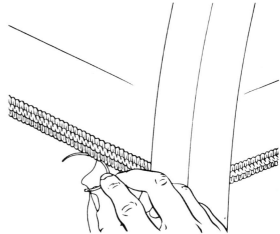

d Sew edges of braid to covering.

Alternatively, you can finish the top cover with a double pleat. Draw the material down over the corner, leaving two folds of excess material, one at the front and one at the side. Tuck the excess neatly away, along the front and the side respectively, behind the facing part of the material, using the flat end of the regulator. Trim off the excess. You will now be left with two pleats, both of them shorter, because of the way the material falls, than the pleat on the single-pleated treatment. Now tack the material securely in place on the underside of the frame.

Finally, trim all round with a suitably coloured braid.

To fix it in place, pin one end to the chair as shown in [4.17] with gimp pins. Hold the braid well away from the chair, and sparingly apply a fabric adhesive. Take care not to spoil your material by getting unwanted glue on it. Carefully press the braid into place with your fingers, working round the chair. Cut the braid when the line meets wood, for example at the back uprights. Finally, with a curved needle and suitably coloured thread, sew the top and bottom edges of the braid to the material, using small, almost invisible stitches.

All that remains is the optional step of covering the underside of the chair with a square of black lining, tacked in place exactly as it was on the drop-in seat.

4.18   Names of the component parts of a chair frame may vary considerably according to the detailed design of the frame, and among different upholsterers. However, the terms used here are generally accepted and widely understood.

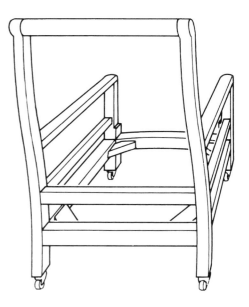

A SPRUNG CHAIR

Start simply and choose, if you can, a small chair with a plain back and springs in the seat only.

If you have no chair of this kind, but only one with a sprung back as well, the process is slightly more complicated and you should read this chapter through, fit the springs to the back as described on page 127, then return to the beginning of the chapter to follow the procedure for fitting the springs to the seat.

If you have to start work on an elaborate item, such as a winged armchair, refer to page 114 to see how to upholster the wings, then return to this section to work on the rest of the chair.

A simple sprung chair has been chosen because much of the work on it is exactly the same as that already described. The only unusual feature is the sprung front edge, which is not used on many chairs. You can either install one, or build the hard edge directly on to the frame as in the stuffed-over seat.

Bear in mind that even chairs of the same type vary vastly in the detail of their construction. You will have to decide how to adapt the processes described here to fit your particular chair. Taking one cautious step at a time, you will soon be able to tell when you have completed a stage correctly.

First strip down the old chair in the usual way. It will be helpful if you can photograph or make a sketch of the chair before you start to remove the old coverings. If you can possibly take them off cleanly, one at a time, you will also be able to record the constructional details of each stage.

When you have removed the old upholstery and springs, make good all the joints. Steam them apart if they are the slightest bit creaky, and re-glue and cramp them. Strip down all the old show-wood, unless it is in perfect condition, and re-polish by one of the techniques described on pages 46–57. Most importantly, fill in all the holes left by the tacks of previous upholsterers. And make sure the edges are bevelled to take the tacks for hard edges all round.

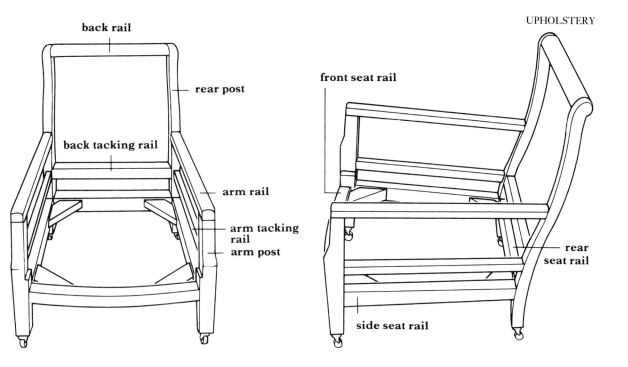

Study the chair carefully. Look at each of the parts in turn [4.18]. Start with the back. You will see that it consists of four members, the two uprights, the top rail, and a piece of wood across the bottom called the bottom tacking rail. The seat also has four members, the front and back rails, and two side rails. Each of these sets of four parts forms a frame, not so different in many respects from the frame you have already learned to upholster on the drop-in seat and the stuffed-over seat. If you can picture these parts of the chair as separate entities, you will have gone a long way towards clearing up the confusion that faces many beginners and makes the prospect of re-upholstering a chair so daunting.

The arms are slightly more complicated. On most chairs they have only three wooden parts – the tacking rail at the bottom, the arm itself at the top, and the front face of the arm. The fourth part, which would form a rear tacking rail, is missing. All it needs is a simple substitute, described below.

As you look at the chair, visualising how the various parts separate out, you must settle the question of which part to begin work on. There is always a great temptation to finish the seat first. Avoid this. If you install the springs in the seat too early, you will find that working on the back and arms becomes almost impossible.

The best procedure is to work on the back and sides of the chair first, taking them to the point where you are ready to apply the first stuffing before you fix the seat springs in place.

First, as in the drop-in seat on which you began, you must fix the webbing in place.

On the back, the position of the webbing depends on two main factors – the shape of the back itself, and whether it is a sprung back. Back springs are soft and flexible and give the seat a gentle, soft feeling. A back without springs but properly stuffed, gives firmer support. Springs are almost always used on very big chairs, so the chair's size may determine your choice. Perhaps the best guide is to restore the chair the way you found it, with or without springs.

81

rear arm 'post'

4.19a Apply the webbing, including a folded strand to form a rear arm 'post'.

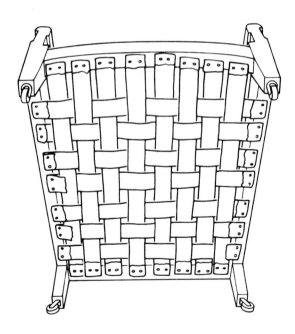

b Fit plenty of webbing to provide a firm base for the seat upholstery.

If you are installing springs in the back of the chair, first apply webbing as in [**4.19a**]. The side-to-side webbing strands fit on the *outside* edge of the frame. Then the upright strands are fixed to the *front* of the frame. This draws the webbing slightly forward so that the sprung back does not show as an unsightly bulge when the webbing ultimately begins to sag in use.

In the small chair illustrated, the back is not being fitted with springs, so the webbing is tacked on to the front edge of the frame. In this chair, the back has a pronounced curve, so it is advisable to fix strands of webbing side to side only. Any webbing fixed top to bottom would tend to even out this attractive curve. And since the webbing will take only moderate pressure, the single strands will be strong enough to take the strain.

You can fix the webbing to the seat itself at this stage. It will not get in the way of any of the work you have to do on the sides and back. You will be using springs in the seat, so the webbing is fixed to the underside of the frame. Use strong 15mm improved tacks, set in the usual staggered 'W' pattern, and pull the webbing taut with your webbing stretcher. The tacks should sit centrally over the frame member to give the greatest possible strength.

The general layout of the webbing will be similar to that used on the drop-in seat, but may vary slightly, according to the number of springs you use. The aim is to get the springs to sit squarely on the webbing.

It makes sense to apply plenty of webbing. It is not expensive and since you are doing the work yourself you can afford to spend a little more time on this part of the job. If using the springs in the 3-3-2 pattern shown in the illustrations, one strand will have to go down the middle of the seat frame.

A useful variation employs doubled strands, the two lengths of webbing lying about 13mm apart, one central pair and others at about mid-point between the centre strands and the outer frame. Keep these strands of webbing parallel and ignore any widening effect towards the front of the seat. The two rear springs should then lie fixed between the centre and outer strands. The position of the springs must also relate exactly to the front edge springs. The main seat springs should lie in line with the gaps between the two front edge springs. Place the webbing as accurately as possible. Diagram [4.20] shows the springs arranged in a 3-3-2 pattern and twine fixing them to the webbing.

Apply the side-to-side strands next, weaving them between those already in place. Do not locate the two rear springs too close to the back of the chair. They will give little support there and their usefulness will be lost under the stuffing of the chair back.

You will probably find a rough sketch plan of the webbing and spring position useful in these early efforts.

Finally turn to the arms. These do not have to carry any weight at all, so a couple of short lengths of webbing running vertically will be enough. However, there is a complication. Since the rear part of the arm does not have that fourth tacking rail, you will have to create a rail to fix the various layers of material on to. Take a length of webbing, long enough to run from the bottom tacking rail of the arm to the arm itself. Fold it

double along its length and tack it to the arm, top and bottom, about two inches from the back upright and parallel to it. This will give sufficient support for the stuffing on the inner sides of the arms.

Now apply the hessian to the arms and back. Fold it over at the edges and tack it down along the line formed by the ends of the webbing strands, using 13mm improved tacks, at 25mm intervals.

On the webbing post you have fixed to the arms, sew the hessian in position. Use upholsterer's twine and any convenient upholstery needle.

Next sew the rows of bridles (or stuffing ties), into the hessian of the back and arms. Pull the twine tight enough to cover three fingers, as usual, starting the row with a slip knot and ending with several half-hitches to prevent the work coming undone. By now you should be able to judge the kind of pattern to use for your bridles. Since these bridles are designed to stop the stuffing sliding vertically down the inside of the chair, you will benefit from having more rather than fewer.

Now place the scrim on the chair arms. Normlly you would fix the stuffing to the chair before the scrim, but you must change the order of operation on this occasion to allow convenient access. With stuffing on the arms of the chair, you will not be able to fit the springs to the seat so easily. And if you fit the springs first, you will have difficulty wielding the hammer to fix the scrim to the bottom tacking rail of the arms. So tack the scrim to the bottom tacking rails, and a short way up the arm at the front, and sew it to the rear webbing upright already made.

Check the dimensions of the scrim for the arms. The pieces must be cut generously, at least 150mm of extra height and 75mm of extra length, front to back, because the scrim will cover the inside of the arms, the stuffing on top, *and* the outside of the arms, before being tacked in place. Cut the two arm pieces together so they match.

Also cut the scrim for the back, and tack it in place along the tacking rail and 100mm or so up the back uprights.

Temporarily tack all three panels out of the way on top of the arms and back. Then begin fitting the springs to the seat.

Fitting the springs

The chair illustrated, like many of this size and type, has two sets of springs. A group of eight lies on the seat itself. And at the front, quite separate, is a line of four smaller springs, fixed to the front edge of the frame and linked together with a piece of malacca cane.

First determine whether any of the old springs can be re-used. To test a spring for wear, stand it upright on a firm level surface and cover it with the palm of your hand. Now press directly and firmly downwards. If the spring tends to tilt over and collapse, or bows outwards at the centre, it should be replaced. Some springs remain even but are simply weak. Imagine it, along with its fellows, taking the weight of your body. Do you think it could? If not, replace it.

Do not replace only one, two or three springs from the front edge. Because of the way they are lashed together, they will all have worn at the same rate and you may find them stronger than some of the rear springs, and be able to save them. But if you decide to replace any, replace all four. This will give a far better finished article and prolong the life of the restored chair.

The length of the springs is important. When they are in position, all of them should lie with their tops at the same height. So the front edge springs, when compressed, must be shorter than the main springs, by the depth of the front member of the frame. Do the simple subtraction sum before you go to buy the springs, but remember that the front edge springs will carry less weight, and will be compressed less. They can therefore be even shorter than the calculated measurement.

Your best guide is an old spring. Take one of each – front and seat – for your supplier to match. He will produce the right length and the appropriate gauge. Failing that, you can use the table below as a rough guide.

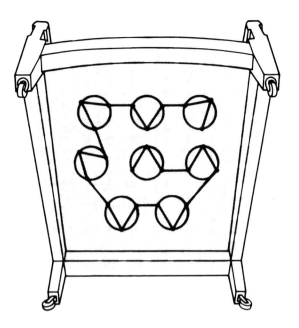

4.20 The seat springs, under tension and lashed securely together, give the chair its basic comfort.

	Seat	Front edge
Sprung stuffed-over seat	150mm	
Small armchair	175mm	125mm
Wing chair	200mm	150mm
Deep armchair or chesterfield settee	250mm	200mm

Next, determine where the springs should be located.

Set out all twelve springs in position first. If you did not keep a note of where they were located follow this pattern: place the four lighter springs on the front edge, the outer ones 50mm in from the arm posts, the other two evenly spaced between them. The front of the springs and the front edge of the frame should coincide, so that the springs overhang the back of the frame.

The seat springs are located in a 3-3-2 pattern, going from front to back. The first two rows should lie in line with the three spaces between the springs in the front edge. The rear two springs will then lie in line with the spaces in the two front rows. The layout is shown in [**4.20**].

When you are satisfied that the seat springs will give all round support to the chair user, mark their positions with chalk on the hessian.

Turn the chair over and sew the springs to the webbing. Start with the centre one, hold it there, and with your curved needle and twine, sew a loop through the webbing and round the metal base of the spring. Tie it in place with a simple knot. Move obliquely across the base of the spring, sew another stitch and knot it. Then go across for a third stitch and knot, so that the spring is held in three places, and the twine forms an equilateral triangle underneath the webbing. Do not cut the twine, but move on to one of the outer springs. On each of these outer springs make sure that the metal join at the top, known as the 'knuckle', points towards the centre. This will help to preserve the balance. Sew the spring in place with three knots, and continue this process until you have gone all round. Knot off the twine firmly after the last stitch [**4.20**].

Lay a length of webbing down over the bottom coils of the four springs along the front edge and tack it firmly home with 13mm improved tacks, two tacks on each side of the wire at each side of the spring. Remember to make the front of the spring and the front of the frame coincide. And make sure that the knuckle at the base of each spring is towards the back of the chair.

Now all these springs must be lashed in place. The purpose is to hold them in position and to ensure that they all move in unison in response to the weight of the sitter. Otherwise, one spring might depress where the pressure is greatest, leaving the others to form uncomfortable edges. It would also cause serious problems if one spring should be forced out of position and unable to return to its correct place.

You will need a ball of 'laid cord' – a soft but strong cord designed specifically for this purpose. Do not use twine. It is too thin to stand up to the pressure of the metal springs. You will also need a supply of 15mm improved tacks, or 15mm wire staples.

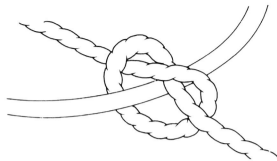

4.21a Locked loop.

b Half-hitch.

As you will see from the illustrations, the springs are lashed together by knotting the laid cord on to them at the front and back of each, at various points up the coils. You will be using knots which may be new to you.

Standard upholstery practice is to knot the first side of the spring with a locked loop, then the second side with a clove-hitch. Some upholsterers use a half-hitch on the second side.

The locked loop is simple. Just take the leading end of the cord over the coil and back under, over the cord itself, under the coil, and away [**4.21a**].

The half-hitch is also simple. Run the leading end of the cord over and back under the coil, then roll the end over and under the taut part of the cord. It is exactly the same as the first part of tying a shoelace [**4.21b**].

The clove-hitch is slightly more complicated but far more elegant. Take the leading end over and back under the coil, and bring it up on one side of the taut part of the cord (properly called the 'standing part'). Then take the leading end over and under the coil again, and back up on the other side of the standing part. Keep this second loop loose. Now pass the leading end through this loop you have formed, and away. Draw the knot tight [**4.21c**].

It is satisfying to abandon the locked loop and the half-hitch, and tie the clove-hitch to both parts of the spring. It takes no longer and gives a far more secure feeling to the entire spring structure. The only disadvantage is that it is more difficult to loosen to adjust. So you will have to compress the springs to the right tension first time.

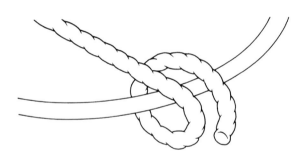

c Clove-hitch.

There are two ways of compressing the springs. One is to tie on all the knots loose, then go back and compress each spring in turn, adjusting the knots and drawing the cord tight as you go. This is rather fiddly.

A better way is as follows. Put your fingers and thumb on the spring at the two points where the knots will be. You will see where this should be shortly. Push down to compress the spring to the required depth. Steady your elbow on the frame to hold the spring in this position, and bring the laid cord to the position of the first knot, as taut as possible. Slide the cord under your finger or thumb, release the other side of the spring, and pinch the cord and spring together. Now, so long as you keep the cord and the spring pinched tight, you can let the spring come out of position, while you tie the knot. Slip on the two loops of the clove-hitch, draw them tight, and relax. When you pull the cord taut again the spring will come back to the right position, determined entirely by the length of the cord from the anchor point where you started to the knot you have just tied.

Go across the spring and tie the next clove-hitch on the other side. Now go to the next spring. The key to this method is that you need not compress this spring at all. It will lie the same distance from its neighbour at the top as at the bottom. All you have to do therefore is judge the length of the cord between them, lean the spring over, and tie the knot that distance away. In practice it will help if you check the right lengths for the lashing, by pressing the two springs down together with a small piece of board.

Lashing the springs remains a fairly difficult job, so do not be afraid to work out some of your own variations on these basic techniques. Any methods that you find comfortable is permissible, providing it achieves the right end result.

You may also find it difficult at first to judge how far to compress the springs. Generally, however, if you have selected the right spring you can depress it about 40mm and not go wrong. Remember that the seat will take about 50mm of stuffing above the top of the springs, so if you can visualise how you want the finished seat to look, and subtract the thickness of the stuffing, you should know how high the top of the compressed spring will lie.

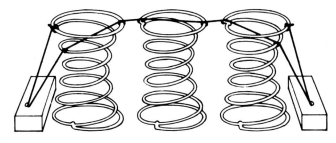

4.22   Lashing the seat springs.

Start by lashing the two seats springs that lie on the central line of the chair from front to back. Cut off a length of laid cord, long enough to run over the top of the springs from the front to back rail, plus half a metre to spare.

Knock in a 15mm tack on the front edge rail. It can be on top of the rail between the front edge springs, or down on the inner side of the rail, whichever is more convenient. Knot the laid cord round it 300mm from the end. Bring the other end up, compress the first spring, and knot the cord to the coil next to the top, with a clove-hitch. Now take the laid cord across to the opposite side of the spring and tie it to the top coil.

Compress the next spring and lash the cord to the near side, on the top coil. Go across that spring, to the coil next to the top, and lash on the cord with a clove-hitch.

Take the laid cord down to the back rail, knock in a tack and tie the cord to it. Lastly, take the two ends of the cord, bring them back up to the top coil of the nearest spring and tie them on [4.22]. The path of the cord – running to a point part way up a spring, across the tops, part way down, out to the tack, then back to the top – holds all the springs in their correct positions.

Securing laid cord to a tack can be difficult; you can make a sturdier anchor point with a proper 15mm wire staple. Knock the staple half-way home and pass the cord through it. Draw the cord to the correct tension and then knock the staple in the whole way. Then tie a half-hitch in the cord to hold it fast. Remember that staples are more difficult to remove than tacks, so get the tension right before you hammer them home.

Go on to the other springs, lashing down from front to back first. The single springs, at the rear of the seat, will have lines of cord of their own, running directly to the top rung of the spring at both front and back. Then lash the springs from side to side by exactly the same method. Finally, put in a couple of lashings diagonally. The whole seat should then look as in [**4.23**]. If any springs are seriously out of line, take off the cord and do them again.

For your first effort, aim to get the tops of the springs lying in a perfectly flat plane. The tops should be level with the tops of the front edge springs. When more practised you could improve the 'set' of the springs by adjusting them to form a slightly domed shape. Then they will take up the weight of the sitter without dipping quite so much, and add to the comfort of the finished seat.

Now lash the front edge springs, front to back first. Cut a length of cord about half a metre long. Tie one end to the bottom coil of the first spring, at the back where it overhangs the seat. Bring it up to the top of the spring. Compress the spring to level with the top of the seat springs, and at the same time draw it forwards about 25mm so that it overhangs the frame itself, and knot the cord round the top coil. Bring the cord to the front of the spring and knot it again. Finally, bring the laid cord down the front of the spring, compress the spring by the right amount, and secure the cord about 25mm down on the front of the frame, with a 15mm tack or staple.

Compress and lash all four front edge springs by this method [**4.24**].

Now lash the four springs together with cord laid from side to side. Cut a length of cord about one-and-a-half times the width of the chair. Secure one end of it down in the corner where the front edge meets the arm post, using either a staple or the tack-and-loop method. Take the cord to the bottom-but-one coil of the first spring, and lash it on. Now take it across the spring to the next coil up, and lash it on. Go on to the second spring. Lash the cord to the top-but-one coil, and go on to the top coil for the final knot. The cord should follow a steadily rising path through those two springs. Go across to the next spring, knot the cord and start downwards, knotting the cord on as you go until you emerge at the corner opposite to where you started.

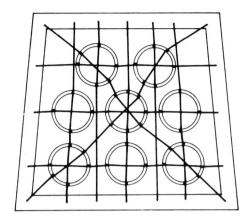

4.23 Pattern of the seat-spring lashings.

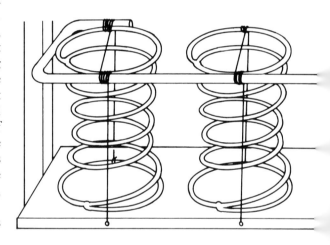

4.24 Front edge springs: lashed front to back independently, and to the cane.

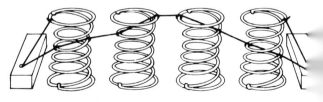

4.25 Side-to-side lashing for the front edge springs.

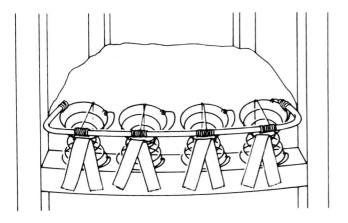

4.26a Add webbing to front edge springs.

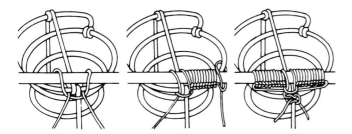

4.26b Detail of lashing of front edge spring to cane.

Adjust all the knots if necessary to make sure all the springs are upright, then secure the end of the cord, as before [**4.25**].

There is an extra piece of support to ensure that the front spring assembly continues to overhang the front edge of the seat. Cut short lengths of webbing, fold them double, and loop them over the second turn of the spring. Pull them taut and tack them to the front edge of the frame.

Finally, lash all the four springs together to a piece of malacca cane. If you have managed to rescue the old cane while stripping the seat, re-use it. If you can buy malacca cane, measure it carefully to determine where it should bend, and scorch it over a flame at the bending points. The heat will weaken the cane and you can bend it into shape. If you have no cane, use 6mm-section round-steel rod, and bend it to shape in a vice.

Now lash it down to the springs with twine. First make a loop over the back of the cane and spring together, and pass the free ends of the twine through the loop. Then start making hitches in each direction outwards from the centre towards each side. About 25mm in each direction will be enough. Finally bring the two ends back to the centre, and tie them firmly together. Trim the ends. Do this on the front of all four of the springs and at the sides of the two outer springs [**4.26**].

Hessian

With the springs all lashed securely in place, you can fit the hessian over them. (Use the same heavy hessian that fits directly over the webbing on other parts of the chair.) When fitted, the hessian will cover the springs and also fit down in a well or gutter between the front edge springs and the seat springs [4.27]. This allows the two sets of springs to operate independently.

Lay a flexible tape measure over the springs from the rear seat rail, tuck it down into the gap behind the front edge springs, and take it on to the front rail. That determines the length of the hessian. To measure the width, run the tape measure *over* the springs between the two side tacking rails.

Tack the hessian, with 25mm folded in all round, to the top of the tacking rails. Secure the rear first, then the two sides. Do not stretch it too tight over the springs. They must be held under tension by the laid cord lashings, and *not* by the hessian. It might be difficult to hammer in the gap between the seat rail and the bottom tacking rails at the side and back. So hammer the tack in at a slight angle, and tack near to the outer edge.

Cut the hessian tidily into the corners as you go.

The well

When you come to the gap just behind the front edge springs, tuck the hessian down into it to form a valley. Let the front part fall over the front edge springs, but do not tack it down. Cut a length of laid cord 150mm longer than the width of the chair; lay this over the hessian, across the seat inside the well, tie a loop in one end, and tack it to one of the side tacking rails. Draw the cord to a snug fit, but not too taut, and tack it down at the other side of the chair. Use 15mm wire staples for extra security if you prefer.

Next, fold the front portion of the hessian back over the well so that it lies over the seat springs, and conceals the length of laid cord.

Feel through the hessian for the laid cord you have just fixed in place, lying along the bottom of the well. Now you must secure that cord with a number of 'guy' cords. In this case there will be six, two in each gap between the front edge springs. Cut six lengths of laid cord about 250mm long. Thread the first one through the

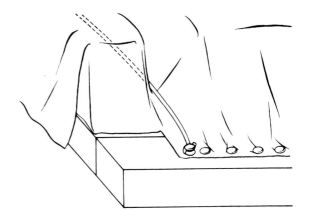

4.27 Cover the seat with hessian, with a strand of laid cord to form the well.

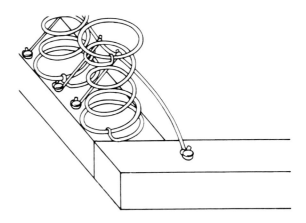

4.28 Fasten guy cord to the laid cord.

weave in the hessian, round the well cord, and out again. You will not be able to thread a needle with the laid cord. Instead, open up the weave of the hessian with the sharp end of your regulator, and push the laid cord through the holes by hand. If you cannot manage this, use the strongest grade of twine that you have and any large needle.

Tie a slip-knot in the guy cord, and draw it tight round the well cord. Then tack or staple home the other end to the top of the front edge, between the front edge springs. The guy cords should appear as in [**4.28**].

When all six guy cords are in place, bring the hessian forward again over the front edge springs, and tack it in place on the face of the front edge of the frame, about 25mm down from the top, and with 13mm of overturn.

You will now be left with a generous fold of excess hessian at each side of the front edge springs. Do not cut it off. Instead push it carefully back between the outside spring and the arm on each side. Form it into a pleat at the top and sew it neatly to the hessian where it lies along the side part of the malacca cane. At the bottom, draw the pleat through and tack it down to the top of the seat tacking rail, just behind the front arm post.

Finally secure the hessian to the seat springs and front edge springs all over. First sew it with twine to the malacca cane, along the front and round the sides. Either use a blanket stitch, working with a curved needle, or sew a series of separate half-hitches.

Now sew the hessian to the seat springs. You will recall sewing the springs to the webbing on the underside of the chair, starting with the centre spring and sewing a triangle of twine with three knots in it, then going on to the others. Sew the hessian to the eight seat springs similarly with a single length of twine. Then sew it to the four front edge springs with another length.

Prepare the hessian to take its first stuffing. Sew bridles into all the areas where they are needed. You may be able to use the securing twine to hold the stuffing if it is not too taut. Alternatively, sew some bridles between the springs. You will also need a few on the slopes round the sides of the seat springs.

You should already have bridles in all parts of the arms, and in the back of the chair.

First stuffing

Now you come to the really creative part of upholstery – stuffing the chair. It has been relatively straightforward on the drop-in seat and stuffed-over seat; simply a question of giving the seat a gentle curve or crown.

On the sprung chair you will have to build up a variety of curves, depending on the style of the chair, its size, and even the shape and taste of the person who is going to own and use it. Part of the value of doing your own upholstery is that you can tailor the seat, arms and back to measure.

As always, the stuffing will be applied in two stages: first stuffing or understuffing; and second stuffing or overstuffing.

The procedure is almost the same as on the stuffed–over seat. On each of the four parts of the chair you must fix stuffing all over, and then cover it with scrim, and secure the scrim and stuffing in place with through-stuffing ties. On most parts of the chair you will build up a hard edge with blind stitches and top stitches. Then you will add the second stuffing into the various dished areas you have formed, and cover them with felt, calico, and finally the top cover.

The arms Start by stuffing the arms. You will recall that you have already partly fitted the scrim, tacked on at the bottom in the form of a 'pocket', to give yourself room to wield the hammer before the springs were put into place. Take handfuls of stuffing from your supply, tease it out and start to tuck it under the bridles. The upholsterer's term is to 'pick' the stuffing over the area. Tuck it down into the bottom of the pocket as well.

Try to visualise how the seat will be when it is finished. The seat and arms will meet and press together, so put enough stuffing down in the bottom of the pocket to make a good contact with the seat later on, when it also has its stuffing in place.

For this part of the operation use mainly fibre or sea grass. Hog's hair is rather expensive to install as the first stuffing in a chair of this size, when the second stuffing will cover it completely. Fibre beds down rather a lot, so put in plenty. When you have picked plenty of stuffing under the bridles, go over the arm again and tuck stuffing in the lines between the bridles, until you have an even covering all over.

Try to visualise how thick you want the arms to be and what shape they were on the chair originally. Keep pressing the stuffing down with the flat of your hand to give yourself an idea of how much it is likely to compress, and to check it for smoothness. You will have to add your one-third in the second stuffing after you have compressed the first stuffing with through-stuffing ties. The hair for the second stuffing will be more expensive, so go on generously until you have a good firm first stuffing as a base.

Also stuff the rear part of the arm generously, near the webbing arm post, as this rear arm edge will not be readily accessible later.

Draw the scrim up over the whole area and put in a line of temporary tacks, spaced well apart, on the top of the arm. Stuff both arms evenly in the same operation.

Now put in a pattern of through-stuffing ties. Thread a straight needle with twine, pass it through one arm near the bottom corner, thread it back, and secure it with a slip-knot. Work in the usual way – along approximately 50mm and through the stuffing, back about 13mm on the webbing side, return the needle, then along another 50mm, until you reach a line near the underside of the arm rail. Finish with several strong knots. Put through-stuffing ties on the other arm.

Next release the temporary tacks. You now have two edges to deal with – the top of the arm and the arm front. Stuff the top of the arm first. This will ultimately be covered with a layer of top stuffing and felt, so you can use mainly the cheaper fibre here. Put a good thick layer on the arm. The filling should eventually be firm, though still giving a comfortable cushion effect.

When you have a good solid layer, draw the scrim over it and tack it with a line of 10mm improved tacks, on the outer edge of the arm, about halfway down.

Now feel the top of the arm. If necessary, push more stuffing in at the open ends and work it along with the regulator. Compare the arm with the stuffed-over seat; it is basically the same job, except that the edge, instead of going along one side then along the other, bends through 90 degrees. In this case you will need a hard roll on the outer edge of the arm. So judge the quantity of stuffing and the slackness in the scrim, to stitch

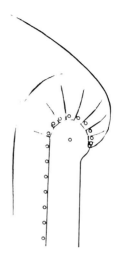

4.29 Pleat the scrim round the arm scroll and tack it down neatly.

in a roll about 25mm in diameter.

Next stuff the front of the arm. If you lay the chair on its side, with the front face of the arm towards you, you will see that it also is almost the same as the edge of the stuffed-over seat. Treat it in exactly the same way.

Start tucking the stuffing material under the fibre you already have in place. This part of the stuffing will form the outer edge of the upholstery; you will be able to feel its resilience through the cover and calico, so try to use best hog's hair here. On each member of the chair, it should make a roll higher than the upholstery in the centre of the arm where the through-stuffing ties are, and should overhang the edges slightly all round.

Go along the inner edge of the arm front, over the top, and down the other side of the scroll to meet the line of tacks you have put on the outside of the arm.

Next, bring the scrim over the roll of stuffing and tack it down all round the bevelled edge of the arm front. As you start to work on the curve of the arm, you have to turn a corner and a great deal of excess material is formed. Pleat up this excess. Fold each pleat over and tack it neatly down [**4.29**]. Both the calico and the outer cover you put on the chair later will have to be pleated

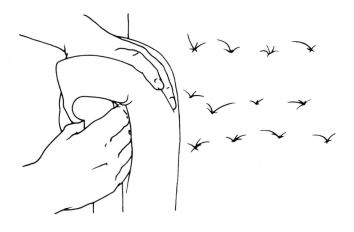

4.30   Tucking in the scrim may help the inexperienced upholsterer to form a neat roll.

in this area, so practise on the scrim to produce a neat job. Arrange the pleats so that they point towards the centre of the arm scroll. Some upholsterers mark this centre with a dot to give them a target to aim for. Too many pleats will produce a series of lumps; too few will leave wrinkles in the material. The main aim is to keep the visible edge of each pleat following a tidy line. Make this outer or top edge of the fold follow the grain of the material. In pleating the scrim it is not difficult, as the weave clearly shows the grain. It can be more difficult on materials like velvets, so any practice you can get at this stage will be worthwhile. Remember to fold the pleats in opposite directions on either arm.

This entire operation – of forming a roll round a tight curve which requires pleats – is one of the most difficult in upholstery. But, there is a way of making it simpler. Form the roll by tucking the scrim underneath the stuffing. Tension and friction will hold it in place and you can go on pushing with your hand until the roll is the right size [**4.30**]. You may find the pleats tend to form themselves, but you will still have to tidy them up with the flat end of your regulator, and make sure they overlap in the right direction. When the roll is the right size, pinch out the scrim near the bevelled edge and tack it through the double layer

thus formed.

Now you need to hold all that understuffing in place, especially at the top of the arms, to prevent it falling down into the bottom edge of the roll. First, sew a line of blind stitches along the top of the arm, starting your needle on the outside of the arm, in contact with the wood of the frame, and pushing it through almost horizontally. Make the usual two anti-clockwise turns of twine round the end of the needle as you pull it back and draw the stitches tight to lock them. As you tighten the stitches you will draw the stuffing firmly down on to the top of the arm frame.

Now carefully sew in a hard edge both round the scroll and along the top of the arm. Apply one row of blind stitches, and one or two rows of top stitches to create a roll about 25mm in diameter. Regulate as you go, to avoid all bulges and dips. The hard edge will follow the gentle curve round the scroll face of the arm, and turn through the angle where the scroll meets the top outer edge of the arm. You should now have no difficulty in making your stitches follow the curve and the angle neatly. Make sure the roll does not form a narrow lip overhanging the edge. Sew the hard edge all round both arms, taking care to match them in all respects.

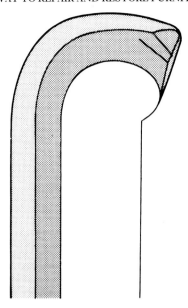

4.31 Sew in a hard edge about 25mm thick with blind stitches and top stitches.

The back Follow roughly the same technique on the chair back. Lay the chair on its back and start to pick your cheaper stuffing material under the bridles. Again you will have a good opportunity to make the shape of the chair fit the most frequent user.

Try to build up a fat padding of stuffing near the bottom of the back, working it into a gently curving hollow towards the top. The fat stuffing at the bottom is called the lumbar swell.

Also sew bridles into the hessian that covers the top rail, and put plenty of stuffing under them. The owner of a good chair should not be able to feel the wooden frame anywhere through the stuffing.

If you have not tacked the scrim on the inside back already, push down the springs, and tack a rectangle of scrim along the back tacking rail. Cut this panel of scrim extremely generously to take

up the curves imposed by the through-stuffing ties and hard edge. Put plenty of stuffing down into the bottom of the pocket to make a good contact with the seat of the chair.

Draw the scrim over the stuffing, temporarily tack it at the sides and over the top, and put in a pattern of through-stuffing ties. The shape you achieve at this stage should give you a clear idea of whether your efforts are likely to be successful. If you have any doubts, don't be afraid to take out the through-ties and adjust the stuffing material.

Release the temporary tacks and begin applying your best quality stuffing material all round the edge, both up the sides and along the top. Fill this area, from one arm, across the top, and round to the other, well enough to make a generous hard edge. [4.31] will show how the hard edge should look at the top. It should oversail the back, and also overhang the sides by a small amount.

Cut the scrim to fit round the arm top rail where it meets the back upright. Between the arm top and the bottom tacking rail you can tack into the front edge of the rear upright, folding the scrim under to give a double layer. Above the top of the arm you will have to tack it to the bevel at the outer front edge of the upright after forming the roll. This bevel should run to the top of the arm, and round any scroll on the side of the arm. Along the top rail, tack the scrim about halfway down the rear outer face.

To make the roll, adopt the same technique as you used on the arms. Tuck the scrim under the stuffing until you achieve the size of roll you want. A 25mm diameter roll edge all round will be adequate. Then pinch together two layers of scrim and tack through them both with 10mm improved tacks. Regulate the stuffing well forward and down against the frame, smoothing out all irregularities as you go.

Try not to leave any temporary tacks in the scrim for too long. With its open weave, scrim tends to slip over tack heads, and they are better hammered home as soon as possible.

At the top corners of the chair back, you will again encounter a curve and an angle coming together. Treat the problem just as you did the arm, and you should have no difficulty in sewing in a neat hard edge, with one row of blind stitches, and one row of top stitches, or two if necessary to make the roll really tight.

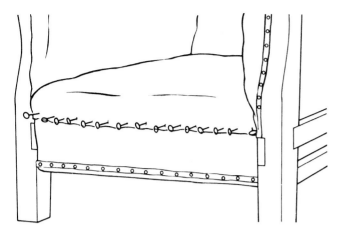

4.32a   Use skewers to hold the seat scrim in place for sewing the hard edge.

The seat Start by picking stuffing under all the bridles, and under the loops of twine that hold the hessian to the springs, if they are loose enough. Continue until you have an adequate layer all over. Be especially careful at the well. You will have to put plenty of stuffing down there, to keep the two sets of springs apart, but not so much that you stop them working independently. On the slopes at the back and sides, put in plenty of stuffing to ensure that you have good contact between the seat and the back and arms of the chair. And make sure you cannot feel any of the springs through the stuffing.

When you have a good even layer, as far forward as the well, cut another generous rectangle of scrim and push it through the gaps at the back and sides. Cut it into the corners where it meets the back uprights, and tack it in place along the top of the back and side tacking rails.

Pack plenty of stuffing above the front edge springs, right up to the malacca cane. Tuck it under and between the bridles. Bring the scrim over to hang down approximately 50mm below the front edge cane. At this point you will encounter another new tool – the skewer. Skewers are quite cheap, and a dozen or so will be enough to cover most upholstery jobs. They are used for holding all kinds of covers in place, where it would be inappropriate to put in temporary tacks. In this instance, use a few skewers to hold the scrim and hessian together just below the cane, along the front face of the seat. Push the skewers through the two layers of material, close under the cane, and up into the stuffing [**4.32a**]. Now sew a pattern of through-stuffing ties on to the top of the seat. You will need the longest double-ended needle you have. You will be sewing through only about 25mm of stuffing, but you will have to handle the needle through the webbing at the bottom of the seat. So turn the seat on its back so that you can see through the webbing. Sew the twine round the top coil of any convenient spring for extra security, but make sure you avoid snagging it round the lower coils, or the stuffing will not be held down tight. Some upholsterers complete the front edge before putting in the through-stuffing ties, which then draw the stuffing down tight.

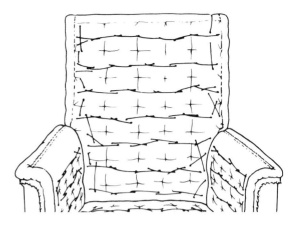

4.32b With a hard edge along the seat, arms and back, and with bridles in place, the chair is ready for final stuffing.

Whichever order you choose, the front will have a hard edge. Aim to make it not more than 25mm in diameter. Make sure you have enough hair in the front part of the seat and bring it well forward with the regulator. There are two or three variations on the method of sewing the hard edge; the following is a standard system and works perfectly well. First, turn about 13mm of the scrim under, and sew it to the hessian with twine using a curved needle. Follow a thread and pull out the skewers as you go. As an alternative, secure the scrim with blanket stitches round the cane.

Check again that there is enough hair in the front part of the seat to form a firm edge. If not, or if the stuffing is not even, add more from the ends and regulate it along. When the front edge is well stuffed, close the ends. Form a small pleat at the corners of the stuffing, and sew it with fine twine to close it securely. Pull the rest of the excess down at the sides and work it as neatly round the arm post as you can. Tack it to the rails at the front and sides, near to the arm posts.

Now sew in a row of blind stitches. Start the needle immediately above the cane. Tuck back any stray hair to prevent it forming lumps around the cane area. Follow it with a line of top stitches. Start them near to the blind stitches, perhaps one or two threads of scrim above, and angle the needle to emerge 40mm back from the front edge. Pull the stitches tight and you will form a neat, even, compact roll, resting firmly on the top of the cane. The chair is now ready for second stuffing [**4.32b**].

Second stuffing

Normally, you would simply cut the calico from your supply as you needed it. But if this is the first large chair you have upholstered, you could use the cutting of the calico cover as practice for cutting the cover itself. So if you are unfamiliar with the procedure, refer to pages 100–2 on planning and cutting a cover, and base the cutting of your calico on it.

The arms Working on the arms first, measure and cut enough calico to run the length of the arm at its longest, from the inside of the webbing post at the back, to the front of the arm, with 75mm at each end for working. Measure the width from the bottom rail of the arm, round the curve, to the underside of the top rail, with a generous allowance for the fullness of the arm. Cut the material square to the weave.

With the chair lying on its side, apply your best quality hair to the inner sides of the arm. Sew in any necessary bridles. On top of the hair, apply a layer of felt wadding, to prevent strands of hair working through the calico.

The main difference from putting second stuffing on the stuffed-over seat is that you can make the arms the shape you want them. You will have to add or remove hair, pulling the calico over it to compress it, until you achieve the correct effect.

Carry on compressing the stuffing and smoothing out the calico with the palm of your hand, as you knock in temporary tacks with the other hand. Use 10mm fine tacks for calico, tacked on the underside of the arm rail.

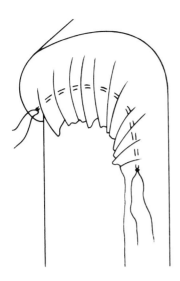

4.33 Pleat the calico neatly over the scroll at the front, and tack or sew it in place.

At the back, pull the calico through the gap between the webbing strand and the back upright. Temporarily tack the calico to the back upright, while you work on getting the arm correctly shaped. When ready, release the tacks, and sew the calico to the doubled strand of webbing, just as you did the hessian and scrim. This will leave a gap open between the arm and the back upright through which the top cover will fit.

When the arm top and the inner arm are neatly stuffed and form fairly straight lines, fix the front scroll permanently. You can pleat the calico as you turn it over the hard edge or you can gather it on a draw-thread.

If you choose to pleat it, use skewers to hold the calico in place. Pleat it exactly as you pleated the scrim, following the grain of the material and folding the pleats down tidily to point towards the centre of the circle of the scroll. Make sure no strands of hair work their way between the calico and the hard edge at that point, or they may cause hard lines under the final cover.

Tack the calico to the facing of the scroll, just inside the tacking line of the scrim. Alternatively, you can blind stitch it to the inner curve of the

hard edge. Use either a straight double-ended needle and twine, or a small curved needle. Make the usual two turns round the emerging point of the needle before you pull it tight.

The other method of finishing the calico is to sew a couple of draw strings into the scroll [**4.33**].

Take an ordinary sewing needle and a length of strong thread. Pull the calico down over the scroll facing and start a line of sewing 25mm in from the hard edge and about 25mm below the point where the edge starts to curve to form the scroll.

Sew through the calico with a running stitch about 2mm long, following exactly the curve of the scroll.

When you have gone right round the scroll, put a knot in the thread. Repeat the line of sewing about 2mm away from the first line, and knot off that thread.

Now take up the two free ends and draw them up to form small gathers, folding the calico evenly over the scroll.

Knot the two threads together at the free ends, put a couple of tacks in the centre of the scroll, and trim away the excess to give a neat finish.

Lastly, hammer home all temporary tacks.

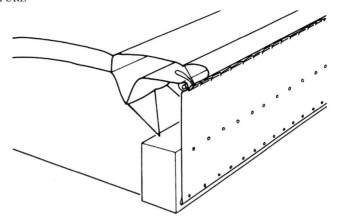

4.34 Section through a seat with platform and first platform at first stuffing stage. The springs are omitted.

The back Lay the chair on its back and sew in bridles both within the back panel and on the top. This is your last opportunity to adjust the shape of the back. If your through-stuffing ties flattened the lumbar swell you created during the first stuffing, use a good thickness of hair in that area to build it out again. When the hair is smooth, well shaped, and firmly secured by the bridles, cover it with a layer of cotton wadding, then calico. Lay the calico over it and temporarily tack at the top and bottom. The tension in the calico should be mostly from side to side. Too much tension in the top-to-bottom direction will tend to pull the curved lumbar swell out of shape.

Draw the calico carefully to the sides and tack it down. At the sides, tack it to the outer face of the side uprights. At the bottom, turn it round the bottom rail and tack it on the outside back. At the top, take the calico right over and tack it on the rear face of the top rail, fairly close up under the roll.

At the arms and bottom rail you will have to cut into the corners. The correct way of cutting at points like this is with a 'Y' cut. Make a straight cut to within about 25mm of the corner, then two oblique cuts right up to the corners so that the material will lie snug. Push the calico through the gaps between the areas of stuffing, and fold the excess under. Work it with the flat end of your regulator if necessary, and tack it down as securely as you can.

The seat Dealing with the seat varies according to the style of the chair. If you are planning to use a cushion on the seat, you will not want to waste expensive material on the invisible area underneath the cushion. In fact, the cushion can often slide on the shiny surface of such materials as hide or imitation leather.

The top part of the seat is therefore made up in two parts, the platform and the front platform [**4.34, 4.35**]. When no cushion is planned or on a small chair, there is no need to divide the seat into these two parts.

There are also several possible treatments for the front of the chair, which is called the border. On a big chair it is customary to divide the material here into two. On smaller chairs one piece is acceptable. It may be finished with a fringe or some other decorative flourish.

The chair illustrated has a seat cover made in three parts: a platform, front platform and a single border. If you want to make a chair with a single-piece platform, simply omit all work relating to the sewing and fixing of the seam between the platform and front platform.

In the arrangement illustrated, start by drawing a chalk or crayon line 180–200mm in from the front edge of the seat, across the width of the chair. This is the line at which the platforms will join.

Now measure the calico pieces for cutting. Measure from side to side on the seat rails, and

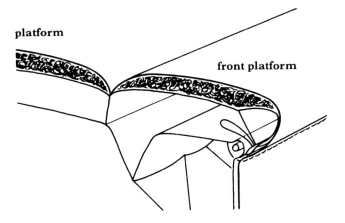

platform

front platform

4.35   The same seat at second stuffing stage.

from the top of the rear seat rail over to the line you have drawn. Add about 100mm for the curve of the top stuffing and for general handling, in each direction. The front platform runs from the chalk line to the underside of the front roll edge. And the border runs from the underside of the front edge down to the underside of the front lower frame, where it will be tacked. Allow a margin of 100mm in each case for general working. When cutting the top cover itself, you will be able to measure and cut to far greater accuracy.

When you measure the front border for width, add 300mm to the measurement across the chair. The calico will have to turn round the front springs, and disappear into the recess between the front springs and the chair arms.

Start by machine-sewing the two pieces of calico for the top of the seat together, and in turn to a piece of tape long enough to run across the width of the chair. Clearly, cutting the calico in two pieces is only necessary if you are practising for later work on the top cover, where a pattern is involved. You can simply make this seam by folding the calico and sewing the tape to the fold.

Now lay the two pieces on top of the seat and turn the platform piece over towards you, to expose the seam turning. Position the seam on the chalk line you have drawn 180–200mm in from the front edge. Working from the centre to the sides, pin it in place with skewers. Now with a 250mm double-pointed needle and twine, sew

through the calico seam allowance, and through the scrim, first stuffing and hessian. Pick up the top coil of a spring whenever you encounter one and sew around it for extra strength, but take care not to snag any of the lower coils of the spring.

Do not pull these stitches down too tight. The aim is to secure the calico in place on the seat, not to compress the stuffing. Stitch through the calico seam allowance only as far as the outer edges of the springs. Do not sew down the sides of the seat. Instead, pull the tapes out at the sides and temporarily tack them to the top of the side seat rails. Now put a thin layer of best hog's hair over the seat as a second stuffing, under and between bridles. Cover it with felt or wadding to prevent the hair emerging through the calico lining.

Push back the panel of calico that will cover the main platform and smooth it out over the seat. Push it down through the recess between the seat and back, and start temporarily tacking along the seat rail, first at the back, then at the sides.

The process is almost the same as for the simpler drop-in and stuffed-over seats. Smooth out the calico to get the tension right, then put in a tack. Watch the weave of the calico to make sure that it goes on straight, and when you have every part well smoothed out, free of bumps and nicely taut, hammer home the tacks.

Now turn the front platform calico back over the main platform to expose the scrim in that area. Again, apply a thin layer of hair to form the top stuffing, bringing it up to the crest of the hard edge, but not over it, or it will form bumps under the final cover. One method of applying the calico now is to bring it right down and tack it on the underside of the front frame member, with no break. On most chairs it enhances the chair's appearance if there is a break just under the lip of the hard edge.

This break is accomplished by sewing a 'banding' in the calico. Make a fold in the calico about 25mm high, and turn the fold up. Adjust it if necessary, and pin it so that the end of the fold butts up neatly against the underside of the hard edge. Now sew the top of the banding in place, using a small curved needle and strong white thread.

The front border is the one part of the chair where there is no first stuffing. So you must put in a few fairly tight stuffing ties, to make a thin even layer on the chair front. You will find it easier if you lay the chair on its back to deal with this part. Cover the hair with the customary layer of cotton wadding to stop the hair working through the calico. Alternatively, you can apply two or even three layers of wadding to the front of the chair, omitting the hair. No-one sits on the border of the chair, so wadding will give soft-looking lines to the chair front and will do the job well. Smooth out the calico of the front border and tack it on the underside of the frame, working as usual from the centre to the sides.

At the sides of the front springing, tuck the calico into the recess as you did the scrim and hessian. Pull it through behind the arms, between the two rails, and tack it to the top of the rail just behind the arm.

The cover

With the calico in place and well smoothed down, the most difficult part of the upholstery is done. Fitting the cover is largely a repeat of the calico covering. The main difference is that as covering fabric is so much more expensive you will have to cut it with great accuracy.

First devise a cutting list, and make up a plot of the seat by drawing a rough outline of each component on it [4.36b]. Then measure from the calico-covered chair, the width and length of each piece. For the typical chair [4.36a] the list will read:

a   inside back
b   outside back
c   seat platform
d   seat front platform
e   seat border
f   inside arm
g   inside arm
h   outside arm
i   outside arm
j   front scroll
k   front scroll
l   piping.

Bear in mind the old saying: 'Measure twice and cut once'. It could save you some costly mistakes. Measure everything with a flexible tape-measure round the curve of the chair, without compressing the calico and stuffing. Measure between the relevant tacking rails. Remember to add 25mm all round each piece for seam allowances and general working.

Inside back Measure the length from the outside of the top rail of the back, over the back, down through the gap between the back and the seat, and round to the rear of the lower back tacking rail. Measure the width across the chair at its widest point, round to the rear faces of the back uprights.

Outside back Measure the width to the outside edges of the frame. Measure the length from under the top rail to underside of the seat tacking rail.

Inside arm Measure the length from the bottom tacking rail over the calico, without compressing it, to the underside of the arm rail. Measure the width from the front of the scroll, through the recess between arm and back, to the outer edge of the back upright.

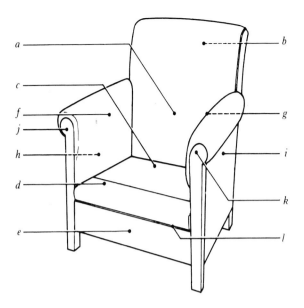

4.36a Cutting list for a typical chair.

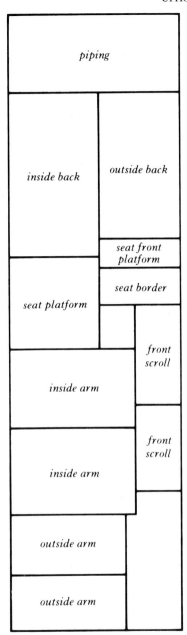

Outside arm Measure the length from the under-side of the arm rail, to the underside of the bottom seat tacking rail. Measure the width from the front outer edge of the arm post to the rear edge of the back upright.

Seat platform Measure the width from the top of one side tacking rail to the top of the opposite tacking rail, at the widest point of the seat. Measure the length from the top of the rear seat tacking rail to the seam you made on the calico cover 180–200mm in from the front edge of the seat.

Front platform Measure the width as on the calico. Measure the length from the seam to the underside of the hard edge, in the position where you built the banding into the calico cover.

Front border Measure the width as on the calico. Measure the length from the underside of the hard edge to the underside of the front lower seat frame member.

Scroll facings Lastly, calculate the dimensions of the scrolls on the front of the two arms.

4.36b Draw up a plot for all the items on the cutting list.

On a chair including curved parts, it might be difficult to obtain accurate measurements. If so, make a template instead. Lay a piece of stiff paper over the relevant surface and adjust to all the curves. Rub round its edge with a soft pencil, keeping the paper firmly in place, skewers will help. Draw a second line outside the first to give a 50mm margin all round. Cut round the outer line and test the template on the chair. Use the template for one arm to produce a matching one for the opposite side.

Now transfer all measurements on to a paper plan. Here you should take into account any design or motif on the cover material.

Make sure you plot all the pieces the right way up. The right way up for a pattern is obvious on the upright parts of the chair. On the seat, consider the back as the top, and the front as the bottom. In other words, the pattern should be the right way up as you stand facing the chair.

Material with a nap, such as velvet, should run 'smooth' down the chair from top to bottom, to avoid trapping dust. The smooth of the nap will then also run from the back to the front of the seat.

Material with a small pattern simply requires that you cut the pieces the right way up, and that the pattern runs vertically true.

If the pattern is large, you will have to work far more carefully to ensure that any dominant motif is centred, otherwise it can ruin the appearance of the chair. Equally, if the top of a motif disappears off the top of the chair and reappears at the bottom, it can make nonsense of the work you have already put into the furniture. Measure the repeat and measure the distance of the motif from the selvedge. Then make a scale drawing. If you cut out the pattern pieces from your cover layout to scale in tracing paper, and lay them over the scale drawing, you will be able to check that your motif falls in the right place.

Start with the inside back of the chair and make sure that any motif is centred laterally, and positioned *just above* halfway up. A motif placed on the true halfway point of the vertical frequently appears to have 'dropped'.

Next, position the seat platform, presuming that you are having no cushions. (If you are, work out the cushions first, again centring the motif.) Also try to plan the cutting so the motifs on the

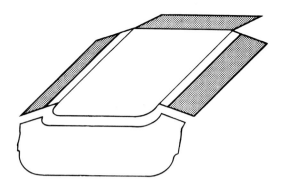

4.37 If the fabric is short or expensive, attach flies to concealed parts of the chair. For example the seat.

seat and back appear the same distance apart as they are on the flat fabric. Of course, you will not be able to do this by cutting the inside back and the seat platform next to each other, or you would have no material to fall down between the two. You will have to achieve this by clever calculation, 'losing' one repeat down out of sight between the back and seat.

There are possibilities of saving material by attaching 'flies' to certain sections [**4.37**]. Flies consist of pieces of hessian, or odd offcuts of material. These occupy parts of the seat that will never be seen, down at the bottom of the inside back, at the rear of the seat platform and at the bottom of the two inside arms. Do not be afraid to use them, either to make your material go further or to give you more play with the designs on the material you have.

When you have laid out the two main parts, plot the remaining pieces. It is important that the inside arms should display the same pattern, or you will upset the balance of the chair. The scroll facing at the front of the arms should also be a perfect match.

Try to match outer arms too. The outside back may not be critical, depending on where the chair is likely to be situated, but if there is any chance of it being seen, it would be attractive to have the motif centrally placed there as well.

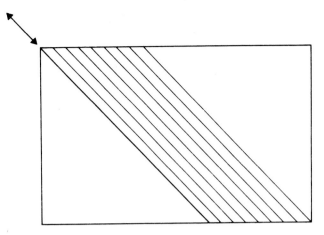

4.38a Cut the piping on the bias.

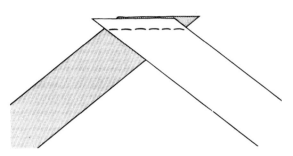

b Sew it right side to right side in a 'V' arrangement.

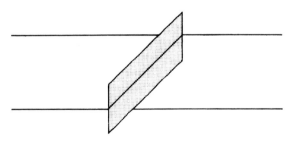

c Open out the fabric and iron the seam flat.

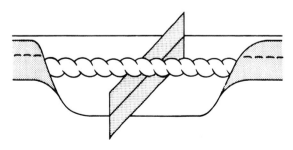

d Sew in the piping cord, preferably on a machine with a piping foot.

Piping This outlines the junctions of the various cover parts all round. You have a choice between making your own pipings or fitting ruche in a matching colour. Piping cord is normally enclosed or 'cased' in the same material as the rest of the chair covering, but you may like to case it in some compatible or contrasting coloured fabric.

Lay out several strips on your cutting plan for the cord casing. They should be cut on the *bias*, i.e. diagonally across the weave [**4.38a**]. The material has more stretch and flexibility when cut on the bias than when cut on the straight grain. A bias helps considerably when bending the piping around curves and corners, at the same time preserving an unpuckered line.

Mark out a line with tailor's chalk across a conveniently wide and long area of the material. Draw other lines parallel to it, 40mm apart. Cut the strips out together with the rest of the fabric.

To construct the piping, first join the strips of fabric. On material with a loose weave, sew a double line of stitching to prevent it unravelling. If you have cut the strips on the bias, place them right sides together in a 90 degree V-shape, and stitch them as shown [**4.38b**]. Then turn the top one over on itself to produce a continuous length. Trim untidy ends and press the seam out flat [**4.38c**].

Next you will need a quantity of piping cord and the piping foot on your sewing-machine. Fold the casing around the cord as you go [**4.38d**] and stitch as close to the cord as possible to produce a firm finish. Roll the piping up until you need it.

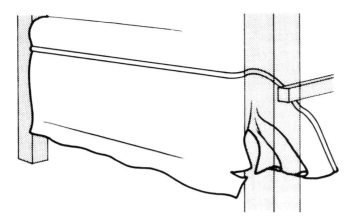

4.39   Pin and try the front border and front platform on the chair until you achieve a good fit.

Cutting the cover

Once sure that you have measured up accurately, including the seam allowances, draw the pieces on the right side of your material. Use tailor's chalk with a sharp edge to draw the outline lightly. Then cut along through the centre of the chalk mark. Do not worry if the material appears to warp as you cut, it will work back into shape when you have finished cutting. Fold each piece sides to centre and lay it safely aside.

Covering the seat

Start by placing, on the seat of the chair, the piece of material cut for the platform. You will recall that it can be either your best material, or, if there is to be a cushion, a piece of lining material.

Take the piece for the front platform and try it in position. The process is virtually identical to fitting the calico cover. The only difference being that calico is normally cut generously and trimmed on the chair. The top cover will be cut far more accurately and you will have to work it into place with precision. When you have done so, measure in from the sides and cut a small notch to mark the exact centre of each of the two pieces of material.

Follow these centralising notches throughout the covering operation.

Now lift the front platform piece over and lay it upside down on the seat, so that the seam edges match. Pin the two pieces of material together, then sew along the seam, at the same time sewing in a length of tape, both to give it strength and to enable you to draw the seam taut across the seat.

Return the platform and front platform to the seat, and lay them in place, but upside down. Draw the front platform over the front edge of the seat and smooth it down over the front and sides.

There will be spare material at either side. Pleat the excess and pin it at each side, as close as possible to the calico lining. Then take the material back to the machine and secure the pleats on the inside with several lines of stitches. Try the cover on the seat the right way up. If you have made both sides accurately it should be a perfect fit, with the two pleats transposed. Trim off any excess.

The material will now lie comfortably down the sides of the seat. If you try the front border in place, you will also have fabric to spare round the sides of the seat. Clearly, the double layer of material is unnecessary, so you will have to sew and trim another join. To make it as unobtrusive as possible, it should be formed as a curved seam, starting at the bottom of the front platform pleat,

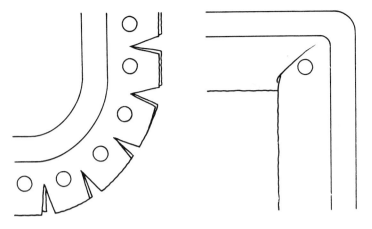

4.40a and b   Cut notches or overlap the seam allowance when turning a corner.

and running down in a curve to the bottom tacking rail. It is almost impossible to cut this curve in situ, so the answer is to cut as far back as you can on the front platform piece with a small pair of scissors, then remove the front platform piece and continue the cut freehand. Now fit the front border to it at the angle the chair will form. Pin them together and try them out, re-pinning as many times as necessary to achieve a snug fit without any strain or gaping. Then cut the front border piece to meet the curve on the front platform piece, with an overlap of about 20mm [**4.39**].

Next, join these two pieces across the front and down the side seams, but this time you will be including a length of piping to give the seam a professional finish.

Check the pieces again to see that they fit well on the chair. Then take them away and turn them inside-out to expose the turnings of the pinned seam.

Working a few centimetres at a time, remove the pins, slide the flat seam allowance of the piping between the turnings of the front platform and border pieces, and re-pin them. Then machine-stitch the whole assembly of four fabric thicknesses together, with the stitch line hard up against the actual piping cord to produce a firm

outline. Check the thread tension on your machine is adjusted correctly to accommodate these extra thicknesses.

To finish the piping, peel back the last 13mm at each end, cut the cord and sew the casing across the end to close it.

At various points you will find you have to take the piping round either an inward or outward curve. If you have cut your casing on the bias this should not prove difficult. However, occasionally a corner is so sharp that you may need to snip the seam allowance of the piping to allow it to bend without stress [**4.40a**].

To turn a corner outwards, mitre the turning [**4.40b**]. This frequently produces too much fabric thickness for a neat external appearance. One solution is to cut the point of the corner off before mitring. Try pressing carefully under a damp cloth for a flatter finish.

Grading seams This practice helps a seam to lie as flat as possible when two or more fabric pieces are joined and need to lie to one side. It isn't necessary if you can open the seam out. This technique is often used when piping is involved. Each piece of fabric within the seam turning is trimmed to a slightly different width and then the widest is pressed down over all of them to achieve a neat finish.

105

The seat cover is now ready for fitting. Lay it in place, starting with the platform. Fold the front platform and the border back over the seat, to expose the seam between the platform and the front platform.

This should now be located over the seam you sewed into the calico cover. Take your 20cm long doubled-ended needle, and once more sew with twine right through the seam turnings, and through all the layers of stuffing, to secure the cover to the seat. Be careful not to snag the twine round lower coils of the springs. Sew across the top of the seat, but not down the sides, and do not pull the stitches too tight or you will compress the top stuffing and form a well. At the sides, tack the tape seam inserts to the top edge of the bottom tacking rail.

Now smooth out the seat platform, and make sure that any motif in the pattern, if there is one, falls accurately in the centre of the seat. Tack the material at the side and at the back to the tops of the respective tacking rails.

Next, pull the front platform piece forward and smooth it snugly over the corners of the front edge springs. If you lift the front border piece, you will expose the turnings of the seam that lies just under the lip of the front edge of the seat, where you folded the banding into the calico. This is the time to check the position of the piping, relative to the front seat rail. It should be at precisely the same height from the bottom of the rail all across the width of the chair. At this stage the piping will be covered by one layer of material, but if you feel for it, and check with a ruler as you go along, you will avoid one of the most unsightly faults in upholstery. As you check the position, secure the material with skewers. Then sew the turning to the upholstery beneath it with a curved needle.

You can now pull down the front border material and tack it to the underside of the frame. Start at the centre, and smooth it out towards the sides, working with temporary tacks until you are sure you have the material neatly in position. Tuck the material away between the front edge springs and the arm. Here you may have to do some careful pleating, in inaccessible places, or even cut into the material to get it to lie smooth.

Draw the excess through behind the arm post and tack it to the side tacking rail.

Covering the inside back

Covering the inside back should present no real problem. If you have done your planning and cutting correctly, the pattern should look right, either following through with the seat itself, or having the main motif falling centrally and slightly above halfway up the back. Remember, the back is the most visible part of the chair and care taken in fitting the inside back cover will be greatly rewarded.

Start by tucking the bottom of the cover down behind the seat and pulling it through to tack the central part temporarily on the top of the lower back tacking rail.

Now smooth the cover material upwards. The tension in the back is particularly important. It is subjected to continual pressure from people sitting in the chair and if not correctly fitted the back will soon sag into unsightly ridges that gather the dirt.

On the other hand, too much tension in the back cover will cancel out the elegant and comfortable curve that you have carefully built into the upholstery.

The way to deal with this problem is to tack the material on temporarily with fairly firm vertical tension. Then stretch it *across* the back with slightly greater tension, taking care not to pull the pattern out of true. Finally re-tack at the top. The sideways tension should then be enough to prevent any creasing. Cut the material to fit round the arm rails, and the tacking rails where they meet the back uprights of the chair. Here, extremely careful cutting is called for. If you cut too short, the material will not lie comfortably round the joints in the wood; if you cut too long, you will produce gaping and looseness.

Above the arms, you will be able to fit the cover exactly as on the simpler stuffed-over seat.

Deal with the pleats at the top corners as with the stuffed-over seat. Smooth the material over the corner, pull the two folds together and sew them with a slip stitch. Alternatively, make one pleat from the crest to the corner, tucking the material away down the sides. Sew up the gap.

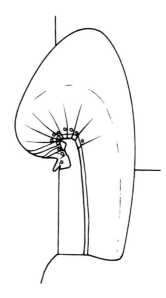

4.41 Pleat the edge of the inside arm cover and tack it round the front scroll.

Covering the arms

It is vital to get the cover material on the arms in the right direction without either creasing or looseness. Fit the fabric from back to front first. Work each stage of the two arms alternately. First lay the covering over the calico and tuck it through the gap where the arm meets the seat back. Smooth it forwards and secure it to the calico and stuffing with a run of skewers, close to the hard edge round the scroll front. Temporarily tack it at the back, on the outside of the back upright. Pull it through the gap at the bottom, and tack it in on the outside of the bottom seat tacking rail. At the top, bring the cover over and tack it on the underside of the arm rail.

Now adjust the cover where necessary to smooth out creases, or to give the pattern a better set. If one arm is vastly different from the other, it is not too late to open up the calico and add a bit more stuffing, with wadding to prevent it working through the covering material.

You will see as you apply the cover, that it is fixed in several places to different tacking rails from the calico that lies beneath it. The calico is fixed to leave gaps between the various parts of the chair. But the two parts of the final cover are fixed to the same part of the frame specifically to close any gaps and prevent objects falling in and being lost.

When satisfied with the lie of the covering material, start to cut into the corners. You will need to cut it where the bottom tacking rail meets the back upright, and where the top arm rail meets the back upright. Tuck the excess material away with the flat end of your regulator. At the front, pleat the material round the scroll, as you did on the scrim and calico. This time, tack the cover material in place all round the scroll and down the front of the arm, about half an inch in from the bevelled edge. Leave the raw edge of the material exposed [4.41].

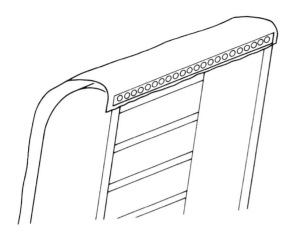

4.42 Back-tack a length of buckram to the reverse side of the outside back and arm covers for a neat finish.

Fitting the outside covers

As it is the outside back which puts the final seal on the visible part of the chair, you will have to install it last. Therefore, do the outside arms first, so that the back can cover their edges. This operation introduces a new skill – back tacking. It is designed to give a straight edge to a junction between two materials.

Turn the chair on its side (protecting the new coverings from damage or soiling), so that you can work on one of the arms. Position your outside arm material over the area it will cover. Then, keeping its upper edge in place, fold it back over the arm.

Now take a strip of buckram, 13mm or 20mm wide, and as long as the underside of the chair arm. Lay it over the two layers of material, with the outer edge of the buckram lying accurately on the line where you want the join to be. Tack through it with 13mm improved tacks, fixing the material in place under it. Now, when you fold the outer arm covering down into place, the buckram will give a neat straight edge [**4.42**].

On large seats you may wish to reinforce the outer coverings with a layer of strong hessian to protect them from behind. If so, tack the hessian under the buckram at the upper edge. You may also find that a thin layer of synthetic wadding gives a soft and well-cushioned look to these outside parts.

Fold the cover material down and tack it, with the hessian and the wadding, on the underside of the bottom tacking rail.

Fold the layers round the front of the arm scroll and temporarily tack them, leaving the cover fabric with a raw edge. You may need to open up this edge later to fit the scroll facings. Cut the fabric to work round the chair leg at the front, and round the back upright at the back. You should now be familiar and perfectly confident with the techniques of cutting the cloth to meet the wood. Trim of all spare material as you go and tuck the folds under with the flat end of the regulator to give a neat finish.

Tack the rear edge of the cover near the inner edge of the rear outer face of the back upright.

Fitting the outside back

On this kind of chair the outside back is straightforward. Add a panel of hessian and perhaps thin wadding for protection, and to soften the appearance, and with a length of buckram to fit across the width of the chair, back-tack the top of the panel. Then begin stitching down the two sides. Use a small curved needle and thread to match the upholstery, and use slip stitch or ladder stitch which will lie concealed under the seam. At the bottom, go right under the bottom tacking rail and tack the outside back cover in place.

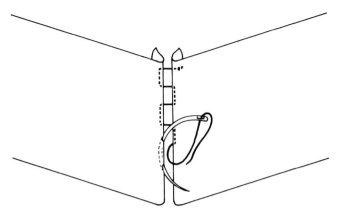

4.43   The slip stitch or ladder stitch forms a neat seam with almost invisible sewing.

How to slip stitch Whenever you have to join two pieces of cover material on the chair itself, and the join will be visible, you sew them with a slip stitch. This gives a neat finish in which the two edges of material butt closely together, and the thread is concealed behind the material itself. It is also called a 'ladder stitch', because the stitches between the two pieces of material resemble a ladder. (American upholsterers call it a blind stitch, but do not confuse it with the blind stitch used to make hard edges in upholstery.)

The technique of slip stitching is the same whether you decorate the seam with piping or not. If you are having piping, sew through the flat seam allowance of the piping cord case to link with the other material underneath it.

If you are sewing two panels together, proceed as follows:

Thread a fine curved needle with thread to match the cover material. Knot the end. At the beginning of the seam, fold one of the fabrics under. Start the needle behind the fold to emerge on its crest. This will bury the knotted end of the thread [**4.43**].

Now take the point of the needle across the gap to the other material. Count back two threads. Push the needle into the material at that point and bring it out 13mm down the seam. Cross back to the first material. Count back two threads, push in the needle on the crest of the fold, and bring it out 13mm along the seam. After you have sewn three or four stitches, draw the thread tight, and rub the seam lightly with your finger.

You will see that the thread completely disappears, running in and out behind the two pieces of material in turn. The reason for going back two threads is to pull the material down tight over the links in the thread, and prevent the stitches showing.

When you come to the end of the seam, if it ends on an accessible part of the frame, knock in a tack halfway, make a couple of half-hitches in the thread round the tack while keeping the thread pulled tight, and hammer the tack home.

If you have to end the seam on a visible part of the chair, carry the stitching back for 50 or 75mm, pull the thread tight, and cut it off close to the material. Rub the seam lightly and the thread will disappear.

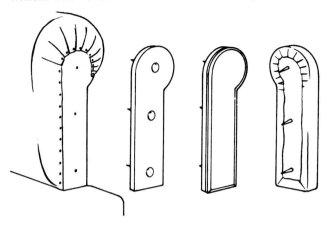

4.44 Fit the scroll front, ready covered, into place.

Making the front scrolls

At the fronts of the two arms you are left with a facing of wood, surrounded by the raw edge of the fabric used to cover the inside and outside arms. If you have stuffed the arms properly they will be a pleasant scroll shape. You must now fill this facing with fabric.

There are several ways of preparing the front scroll facings. The most reliable method is to use plywood. It will be covered with fabric material and surrounded with piping to give a neat finish to the join.

On smaller chairs cardboard may be sufficient, or buckram with two or three layers of wadding to soften it gives a pleasing finish.

The problem lies in fixing the plywood to the front of the chair arm when the material is covering it.

One method is to nail through the fabric with a small-headed nail. If you are careful, you can part the threads of the covering fabric, knock in the nail, then work the threads together and close up the hole in the fabric. This method is obviously not suitable for delicate fabrics, nor for hide or leathercloth.

Alternatively, you might hammer flat-headed nails through the plywood first, then cover it with material and protect the material from the hammer with a large piece of softwood as you hammer home the facing.

Neither of these solutions is as elegant or effective as the double plywood method, although a double layer of plywood might produce too bulky a facing if you have made your arms with very thin stuffing.

First make a template of the facing panel. Hold a piece of paper against the face of the scroll and draw carefully and closely round the line where the face meets the hard edge.

Cut out the template, check it, and trim if necessary. Also check it against the other arm. The scroll facings should be the same size and shape to ensure an even appearance to the front of the chair. If your two sides are different, try to work out whether adding to one and forcing the roll edge out, or leaving a slight gap, will produce the more evenly balanced compromise.

Using the template as a guide, cut out four panels of thin plywood, two for each side.

Now obtain six 25mm flat-headed round-section nails. Find a drill bit with a diameter identical to or slightly smaller than the nail shank.

Offer up a single piece of plywood to the arm facing and drill through it into the arm, 25mm deep in three evenly spaced places.

Push three nails through the holes in the plywood and glue the second piece of plywood over the first to cover the heads of the nails. You may produce a better job if you countersink the nail holes to lower the heads to level with, or just below, the surface of the plywood. Bevel the outer edges of the plywood shapes to remove sharpness.

Now cut your facing material, allowing a 25mm margin all round the edge of the plywood. Take the usual care to match the patterns, and if possible to have an interesting feature of the pattern showing [4.44].

Lay the facing material face down on a clean surface, and lay the double layer of plywood on the material with the nails up. Draw over the edges of the material, snip or pleat them to accommodate the curves, and tack down the material to the plywood with 10mm fine tacks. On a chair of the type illustrated, the scroll facing runs flush with the outer edge of the chair because of the way the hard edge is constructed. On a chair which has a stuffed edge right down the outer side, you will be able to tack the fabric to the plywood all round the scroll facing. On the chair illustrated, tack only round the inside edge. Leave the outside edge open.

Next, prepare some piping, long enough to go round the facing, either all round or as far as the join between the arm roll edge and the outer arm cover. You can choose to close the join between the facing and the outer arm cover with a simple slip stitch. Finish the piping as described on page 105.

Now offer up the completed facing to the arm, and push it firmly home. The nails should match the holes exactly, and should hold the facings in place with a tight push fit. There should be no need to hammer the material, but if there is, protect it with cloth and a large piece of softwood.

Where the outer edge of the facing remains open, tuck it behind the outer arm cover and slip stitch the join.

Sewing on scroll facings

Another method of attaching scroll facings, especially in more modern and softer lines of furnishing, is to sew them on without any stiffened support. They can be decorated with cord, piping or ruche, or be left plain.

First fit the outside arm, temporarily tacking it at the junction with the scroll face. Then, with the chair on its back, cover the scroll face with a thin layer of stuffing covered by wadding. A modern material like synthetic wadding is ideal here, as ordinary stuffing tends to sink to the bottom of the scroll.

Trim the fabric for the scroll 13mm over-size to provide a decent turning and V-shaped notches where necessary to avoid lumpy folds. Do not cut too close to the visible face of the fabric.

Slip stitch the facing fabric into place. If the facing meets the outside arm cover at the outer front edge, release the temporary tacks and fold the fabric of the scroll front under the arm cover. Next fold back the outer edge of the outside arm to give a 13mm underturn. If the turning is greater than this you will risk unwanted folds which will show through the cover itself. Any less will risk fraying. Slip stitch the two together. If you are using piping or ruche, insert it as you go.

Chair cord

An alternative method of concealing or decorating a seam is to use chair cord, a decorative twisted cord that gives a luxurious finish to a chair and saves you the bother of making piping. Of course, you have to be able to obtain it in a colour that will harmonise with your cover, and it can be unsuitable alongside some patterned fabrics. Also, it is difficult to use it where it comes to an exposed end. But where the cord disappears out of sight beneath the frame, or where it comes to a T-junction with another length of cord, it is ideal. It will have to be sewn on with matching thread.

With long dressmaker's pins, pin the cord in place to cover the seam. You will remove these gradually as you sew. Start sewing with a slip knot underneath the end of the cord, buried in the slip stitching below [4.45]. Then sew directly through the cord. Next, insert the needle into the fabric below, underneath the point where the thread emerges from the cord, and make a stitch of about 10mm. At that point, sew back through the centre of the cord and begin another stitch. Draw the stitching taut every so often and the cord will lie quite flat hiding the seam.

Use chair cord at any point where you might otherwise choose piping – round the facing scroll, round the front border, and along the top of the chair back, or completely round the outside back.

Lining

The final task is to add the cover of black lining underneath the chair to keep it free of dust. Install it shiny side out, cutting it carefully to fit round the legs.

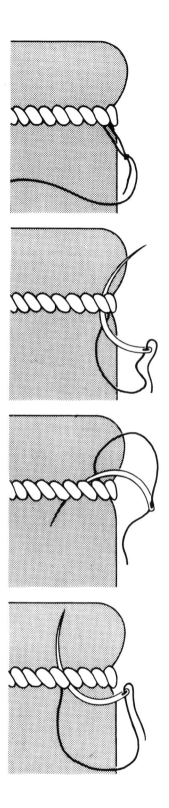

4.45   Chair cord can be sewn over exposed seams as an alternative to piping.

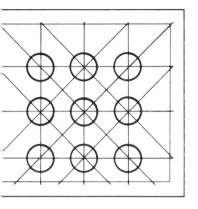
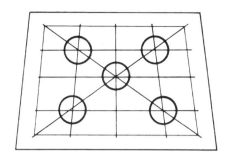
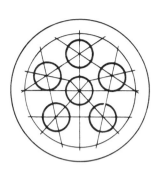
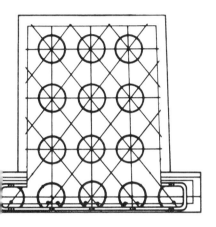
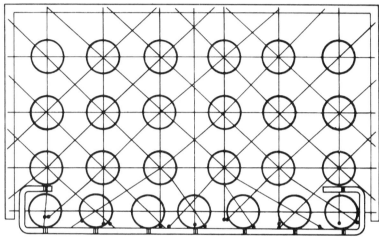

4.46 Alternative springing patterns for various types of seat.

VARIATIONS

Chairs and sofas are so variously designed that it is impossible to give an account of every problem you are likely to encounter. Individual crafts-manship is called for, and any upholsterer must make his or her decisions about the most suitable method of working on any given chair.

However, there are a number of common variations which are considered below. Reference to them and to the basic techniques previously outlined should offer an adequate working guide to most of the jobs home upholsterers are likely to undertake.

Springing patterns

The layout of springs in a seat depends on shape and size. The chair described above narrows slightly towards the back, making a simple 3-3-2 pattern suitable, see [**4.23**].

Other shapes of seat are shown in [**4.46**] with suitable spring layouts. Bear in mind that the side and rear springs should not be placed too close to upholstered arms and backs, where the effect of the spring may be lost under the overhang of the upholstery.

Position springs where possible in straight lines, to make lashing them with laid cord easier and more effective.

113

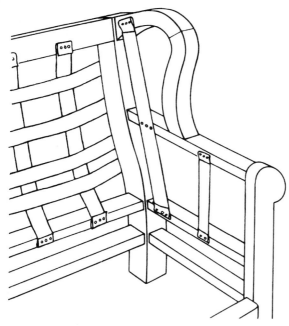

4.47 Build a rear wing 'post' of webbing to take the hessian.

WING CHAIRS

Wing chairs are similar in most respects to the basic sprung chair. Working through the basic chair you learnt to think of the chair as four separate surfaces, three of them unsprung. You only have to think of the wings as a fifth and sixth surface to be upholstered.

First check the type of frame on which you will be building the wing. All wings will have a wing rail at the top and a wing post at the front. They should be well curved to merge together. But these alone are not enough to carry the upholstery. You will need third and fourth sides to form a frame on which to tack or sew the various layers of upholstery. More elaborate chairs will have a wooden slat running from top to bottom near the back of the wing. This forms a gap through which will pass the covers to be tacked on to the rear and outer surfaces of the frame.

If yours does not have such a slat, you will have to make one with webbing. It is simplest if you run the webbing that forms the back post of the arm right up to the top of the wing, more or less parallel with the back upright [**4.47**].

If the wing is large enough, you can usefully add a strand of webbing in each direction, tacked to the inside of the frame to support the upholstery. The wing does not have to carry any appreciable weight, but webbing will make it more solid and durable. Then apply a layer of hessian, tacked on at the top of the frame and round the front curve, and sewn to the upright webbing post you have fitted yourself. At the bottom, leave a gap of about 25mm above the arm rail. Simply underturn the hessian at this point and, for neatness, sew up the underturn.

To upholster the wing, first make sure that the outside edge of the curved part of the frame has a bevel cut on it. This is to take a roll or hard edge sewn into it, exactly as other parts of the chair have roll edges.

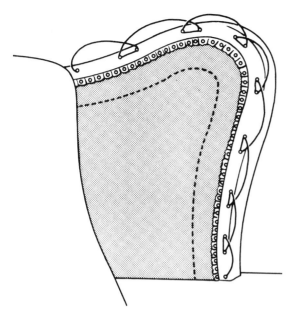

4.48a Tack bridles on the wing outer edge and draw a chalk line on the hessian.

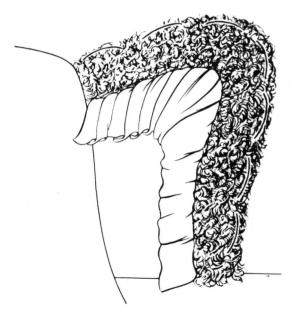

4.48b Sew a band of scrim round the chalk line, add stuffing and tack down the scrim to form a roll.

Producing that roll for a wing is slightly different from building an ordinary seat roll. First, with a piece of chalk, lightly mark the hessian round the curve of the wing, about 75mm in from the outer edge.

Cut a length of scrim, 20cm wide and long enough to reach generously from the arm rail to the top rail of the chair back. Turn the scrim under, and sew it to the hessian round the chalk mark, pleating it as you go. [4.48] shows the building of this type of roll.

Now fix some bridles to the curved wooden frame of the wing. Fix a few tacks round the inner face of the frame, about 13mm in, and loop some twine between them. Pick some stuffing under these loops, and also down between the loops and the sewing line of the scrim. Draw the scrim over the stuffing so that it forms a long curving tube, conforming to the curve of the wing. Adjust the scrim and add as much stuffing as necessary, so that you can turn the scrim under the stuffing ready to sew in a hard edge. Add enough stuffing to produce a hard edge about 25mm in diameter. When you have it taut and well filled, tack the scrim down to the bevelled edge of the frame. You will have to do some skilful pleating as you work round these tight curves.

Work evenly on both sides for visual balance. Do your best to achieve continuity between this roll and the roll across the top of the chair back, and try to produce a good firm junction with the upholstery of the arm. At the top corners of the wings you can either turn the end of the tube under or sew the scrim to the hard edge of the chair back.

Taking care to avoid snagging the bridles, regulate the stuffing inside the tube to give a slight overhang all round the wing frame. Then sew in the 25mm roll with a row of blind stitches and a row of top stitches.

A simpler method, which is acceptable on wings without pronounced curves, is to treat the wing as one area, omit the separate tube, and upholster it with webbing and hessian, bridles all over, first stuffing, scrim and through-stuffing ties. Regulate the stuffing to the edge of the frame and sew in the hard edge.

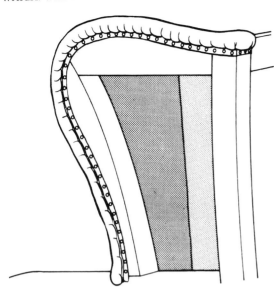

4.49 Sew a hard edge all round the wing, add second stuffing and wadding, and cover with calico.

Stuffing

It is usual to take the arms and back as far as the calico stage before adding the second stuffing and calico to the wings.

When you come to the wing second stuffing, sew some bridles on to the hessian in the area not covered by the stuffing in the tube, and pick some hair under them. Add hair all over, to form an elegant curve meeting the crest of the roll edge all round the wing. Cover it with wadding to prevent the hair working through the covers, and start applying the calico. You will have to make several snips in this piece of material to accommodate the tight curves and frame joints, so do not be dismayed if you have to have more than one go at it on your first wing chair. Start by cutting your calico fairly generously. Make cuts in the bottom of the panel to allow it to go through the gap between the underturned edge of the hessian and the top of the arm. Temporarily tack the calico to the top of the arm.

Now take the calico over the top of the wing and temporarily tack it there. Pull the calico through the gap at the back so that you can temporarily tack it to the back upright. And pull it round the front curve of the wing, to tack it to the outer rail. Be prepared to adjust these tacks several times as you smooth out and compress the calico with the flat of your hand. Pleat the calico on the convex part of the wing curve, and snip the edge so that it follows the concave part of the curve. At the top back, tuck in the calico with the flat end of your regulator to give a good junction with the chair back, and to seal in the stuffing and wadding.

Keep all hair and wadding away from the crest of the hard edge where it would cause unsightly and uncomfortable lumps. Finally, release the temporary tacks at the rear of the calico panel. Turn the rear edge and sew it to the webbing to re-open the gap between the wing and back upright [**4.49**].

The method of dealing with the bottom edge of the calico depends on the style of the final cover. In most chairs the wings are upholstered separately from the arms, to give a seam, either plain or piped. This treatment is elegant and allows you to build interesting shapes into the wings. If you plan to use this method, release the temporary tacks at the bottom of the wing panel of calico, and turn the calico up so that you can sew it to the hessian, to open up the gap between the arm and the wing, ready to apply the top cover. At the same time, make sure you have a good supply of stuffing in the bottom of the wing to ensure that no gaps appear between it and the arm.

Less elaborate styles of chair often have the wing and the arm upholstered in one piece. If you plan this treatment, loosen the calico of both the arm and the bottom of the wing panel. Push stuffing into the opening to make a smooth surface where the two meet. Draw the wing calico down over the arm calico. Underturn the raw edge of the wing calico and sew the two together with a slip stitch.

Covering the inside wings

If you are treating the wings as separate from the arms, it is normal to cover both the inside back and inside arms first. The cover for the wings is then tacked down over them, to the same tacking rails.

First cut the covers for the two wings, ensuring that the pattern is balanced. If there is a pronounced feature, make sure that it sits well on the face of the inside wings. There are at least two ways of treating the wings at the point where the wing cover meets the inside back cover at the top of the chair. One method is to fold both covers under and slip stitch them together to form a mitred joint.

The alternative is to overlap the two covers. Cut the inside back cover in such a way as to leave a 'tab' of material a few inches long, running along the wing and tacked neatly in place. Do not turn the material under or over, as the double thickness will cause an ugly bulge. Then fold the material of the wing under, and slip stitch the two together.

Of course, if you choose to cover the wing before the inside back, you should leave the tab on the wing, and fold the material of the inside back cover over it.

Fitting the cover is then more or less the same as fitting the calico. Smooth the material over the wing, and tack it down first with temporary tacks at the bottom, then at the sides. The main difference is in the tacking rail. Just as the seat and inside arm cover are tacked down together to the same rail to give a smooth run to the material and prevent gaps forming, so the inside arm and wing covers are tacked together, on the outer side of the back upright. Also, the cover material at the bottom is drawn through the aperture, and tacked down on the outer side of the arm rail, giving an almost continuous run with the arm cover itself.

You will have to work the material carefully over the curving roll edge, pleating it and snipping it to follow the curves.

When it is tacked all round, with all the folds and creases smoothed out, add the piping. Generally a wing chair looks best if the piping sits just outside the line of the crest of the roll edge. You will be able to tack it in position, covering the tacking of the inside wing cover itself. The piping will normally run from the junction of the wing with one arm, round the curve of the wing, across the chair back, and down the other wing to meet the opposite arm.

Outside wing cover

It is usual to finish the outside wing covers before the outside back and arm covers. The top of the outside arm cover then overlaps the bottom of the wing cover. The outside back cover will go on last, overlapping the covers of both the outside wing and outside arm where they are pulled round the back upright.

If the wing cavity is a large one, it is advisable to fill it with stuffing – the cheapest type will do the job – to prevent the cover being forced in, stretched and ultimately made slack during use. Fill the cavity with stuffing, then tack hessian over the frame.

If the wing itself has a pronounced shape – and some of the most elegant chairs have generous curves on the outside wings – you will have to add bridles to the hessian, then stuffing, then scrim, and finally a layer of wadding and calico. On this type of chair the frame will probably be built to incorporate these curves, in which case one or two strands of webbing across the wing frame underneath the hessian may help in building up and holding the shape.

If the back upright is to have piping, apply it at this stage, tacking it so that the roll of the piping lies exactly on the crest of the corner.

Finally, lay the outside cover in position and slip stitch it all round, snugly up against the cord inside the piping. When you come to the bottom of the wing you can pull the cover down flat, and tack it to the arm rail, leaving a raw edge to be covered by the outside arm cover.

Once the wing is completed, add the outside arm cover as on the basic chair, back tacking the top edge with a length of buckram. Slip stitch the cover to the vertical piping at the front and back of the arms, and turn it under the bottom seat rail for tacking. Install thin padding or wadding to give a softer look under these outside covers.

Follow with the outside back cover. Back tack this to the chair if you can work buckram close up to the piping along the top edge, then slip stitch it vertically down the sides. Alternatively, slip stitch it all round, and turn it under at the bottom for tacking. Finally, cover the underside of the chair in black lining.

DEEP-BUTTONING

The main difficulty with deep-buttoning lies in getting the right quantity of stuffing in the 'bun' between the buttons. Too much and the pleats between the buttons strain and develop an unsightly gape; too little and the upholstery looks flimsy, lacking the character of a well-crafted luxury article. The worst possible combination is to have uneven amounts of stuffing and covering fabric between buttons, with the result that the job looks irregular and lopsided.

However, any mistakes can only arise from incorrect judgement. The first task is to plan the buttoning. Make a sketch of the parts of the chair which will feature deep-buttoning. It will normally be the back, sometimes the seat and arms as well. Then mark out your buttoning points on the plan.

The shape between the buttons usually takes the form of a diamond. The exact dimensions of the individual diamonds are not critical, but they are generally longer vertically than horizontally. 200–300mm is generally an acceptable height, depending on the size of the chair.

First, consider some typical shapes for the backs of medium-sized chairs.

If the back is almost square, start by drawing a straight horizontal line near the bottom. A good guide to the height of this line above the seat is to take the height of the diamond you plan to use, halve it, and add 50mm. The bottom row of buttons will lie on this line, and the lowest row of diamonds will then sit comfortably rather less than a diamond's height about the chair seat.

Now draw a second horizontal line 100–150mm above that (half the height of your diamond), then another, and so on until you reach the same height from the top as your first line is from the bottom.

Now strike a vertical line down the exact centre of the plan. Add other vertical lines, to the right and left, at a distance that will give well-proportioned diamonds when the intersecting points (where the buttons will be) are joined up. [4.50a] shows a simple arrangement. However, such an arrangement is only suitable for regular rectangular seats. Many seat backs are wider at the top than at the bottom, and may also have a slight barrel shape. So you can improve on the basic shape by drawing the lines with appropriate curves and tapers.

If the chair back is slightly barrel-shaped, the horizontal lines should curve downwards slightly from the centre towards the ends. And the top lines will curve down more than the bottom ones. Start by drawing the bottom line almost horizontal. Draw a vertical centre line and mark off the measurements along it. Then draw the top line parallel with the curve of the top of the chair back. Curve the lines in between them slightly less as they go from top to bottom.

4.50 Deep-buttoning patterns suitable for [a] a square back; [b] a curved back; and [c] a curved and tapered back. Curved [d] and tapering curved [e] backs incorporating vertical channels at top and bottom. Side pleats can also be added.

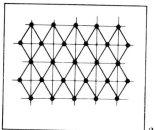
a

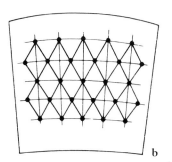
b

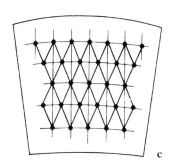
c

You can also vary the vertical lines. On a chair back which flares outwards towards the top, you can either draw the vertical lines to fan out slightly, or you can have more buttons at the top, or both. [4.50b,c] shows these effects.

To get the buttoning points right, first mark the intersection of the bottom horizontal line with the centre vertical line. Then mark the points out along the bottom line in each direction. Mark the next-but-one line up at similar points. And, if you have enough lines, the next-but-one line above that – first, third, fifth lines, etc. Mark the alternating points on the second and fourth lines, and draw in the diamonds to link these points. You will produce a pattern of diamond shapes between the buttoning points.

Be careful how far you extend the points towards the sides. The distance from the visible side of the buttoned panel to the nearest vertical line with a button on it should be approximately the same as the distance between buttons on the nearest horizontal line. Do not button too close to the sides.

On large surfaces, the top and bottom of the buttoning panel often carry vertical pleats which sink down into channels just as the buttons sink down into recesses. If the chair back flares towards the top, it is usual to have one more channel at the top than at the bottom. These patterns are shown in [4.50d,e].

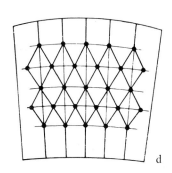
d

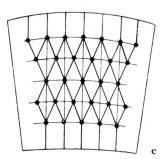
e

Measuring the cover

Consider first the process of deep-buttoning a chair back without springs. First, install the webbing, hessian, first stuffing and scrim.

Put in some through-stuffing ties, then add some bridles to hold the second stuffing in place. The buttoning itself will do most of the work of keeping the stuffing in place. In fact, the original reason for inventing deep-buttoning was to hold stuffing on chair backs in place without it slipping. But stuffing can easily be dislodged during the actual process of buttoning, so the bridles will help maintain the regular shape.

Pick some best quality stuffing under the bridles, and then between them, until you have the required thickness. In general, a thickness of 40mm–50mm, when the stuffing is compressed, is about right. But the thickness depends to a large extent on the style of the article, and on the firmness or softness required. Thicker stuffing is usually softer; thinner stuffing generally more firm. You will have to use your judgement, compressing by hand and trying to imagine how the finished article will look and feel.

Now cover the stuffing with a layer of cotton wadding, ready for installing the calico cover. This will give excellent practice for working on the final cover.

Refer to your buttoning plan, and mark the buttoning positions on the back of the chair. Push skewers through from the back at these positions. From the front of the chair, carefully feel with your fingers for the points of the skewers to determine the position of the buttons. Now tear a neat hole in the wadding, and push away the stuffing behind it with your regulator or your fingers, to make a recess in the stuffing running right back to the scrim cover.

Next, you will have to determine the measurements for the calico and outer covers. They will be different from the original button plan, to accommodate the curves of the 'buns' between the buttons. And, of course, on any given seat the measurements for all the buttons may not be the same. They will vary slightly if you have incorporated curves in your original lines. And they will vary according to the pattern of curve in the chair surface – less for a concave surface like the barrel-back of the chair, considerably more for the convex curve of something like a chesterfield.

That is one source of difficulty in deep-buttoning.

The easiest answer is to work with a second paper plan. Start with a sheet of calico big enough to cover the chair back and to take up all the curves of all the buns, plus a generous margin for error. Draw the bottom horizontal line of the button plan on it, following a thread if the line is straight. Now, on the chair, measure from that line to the bottom tacking rail on which the calico will be fixed. Take all measurements for this stage with a flexible steel tape measure. Push it down into the button hole as far as the scrim and bend it to follow the curve of the stuffing when the stuffing is compressed. Transfer that measurement to the second paper plan. It will give you the bottom tacking line. Take the measurements to the next button line, and the next, working up the centre of the chair. Then work towards the outsides. Accommodate all the curving lines as you go.

Go on taking the measurements until the cover plan is finished. Make small holes in the paper, and mark through them on to the calico. Keep your plan to mark the final cover.

Now lay the calico over the wadding. Tuck it into the recesses in the stuffing along the bottom two rows of buttoning points. At the buttoning points on these two lines, sew the calico to the base through the scrim, first stuffing and hessian, using either strong thread or fine upholsterer's twine. Tie it at the back with a slip-knot.

The reason for sewing only two rows at first is that you will need access to the insides of each diamond for adjusting the stuffing, and for setting the pleats.

First, adjust the stuffing if necessary, to ensure that you have the right degree of fullness, as far as you can judge it. Put more in or take some out, but try not to disturb the wadding. Then put in the pleats between the buttoning points you have so far sewn down. You will need the flat end of your regulator and some other similar instrument. Another regulator is ideal. Failing that, an old kitchen knife or the handle of a spoon will do. Push one flat blade under the calico to ease out the fold of the top of the pleat. Push the other blade into the pleat from the top of the calico. Hold the two blades lightly pushed against each other, and draw them along the pleat between the

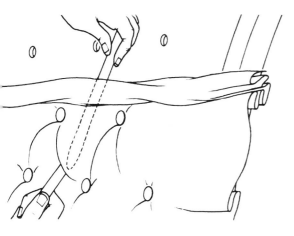

4.51a Use a regulator and another similar tool to form a smooth pleat between buttoning points.

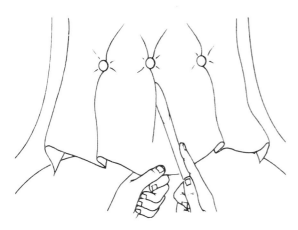

4.51b When the buttons are fixed, form the channels to the top, bottom, and sides of the frame.

buttoning points. This will take up any slack and leave you with a well-formed flat pleat [**4.51a**].

Remember that all pleats on a deep-buttoned surface must face downwards, to prevent the open side of the pleat from forming a dust trap. Arrange the pleats in the calico to fall the same way.

Go on to the next row, and sew the calico to the base at the buttoning points. Check the stuffing and ease out the pleats. Go on and finish all subsequent rows.

With the calico well fixed all over the central part of the panel by these buttoning points, you can deal with the sides. Their treatment largely depends on the design of chair. Refer again to your first buttoning plan. Did you incorporate channels running from the top and bottom rows of buttons to the top and bottom rails? If so, make the channels exactly as you made the pleats between buttons [**4.51b**].

Catch about 20mm of the calico, and form it into a pleat. Temporarily tack it on the relevant rail.

Finish the channels all round, and when you have eased out all the creases and wrinkles in the calico, tack it down with 10mm fine tacks, leaving a raw edge.

Now take up the cover itself. Recall the way the calico went on, and make any necessary adjustments in the measurements between buttoning point, and the measurements from the sides, top and bottom of the frame. Lay the fabric face down on a clean surface, and place the second paper pattern over it, amended as necessary. Carefully push the point of your regulator or sharp skewer through the pattern at the buttoning points, and right through the material to leave a small hole that will show on the face of the fabric. Where the pleats or channels meet the sides, top and bottom of the frame, cut a small notch. You are now committed to fitting your buttons in the positions marked.

The buttons

What of the buttons themselves? The only way to produce buttons of the type needed is to buy button bases and cover them yourself in the material you are using to cover the chair. Button bases come in two parts, with various types of fixings. You will need the looped variety.

To make up the buttons you will need a button-making tool. This will cut a small circle of material for you, and in a simple quick operation install it on the button base, then press the sections of the base together to complete the button.

It might be worth buying one if you are planning to do a great deal of this kind of upholstery. Alternatively, you might be able to find a professional upholsterer who would be prepared to make up a few buttons from your own material quite cheaply. Some department stores will make up buttons for the home upholsterer; ask at either the haberdashery or upholstery departments.

Fitting the cover

Once you have the second stuffing and calico installed, the remainder of the operation is relatively simple.

Take your cover, buttons, a medium-length double-pointed needle, and a one-metre length of medium twine for each button.

Start at the centre of the bottom row. Drape the material over the chair so that the holes coincide roughly with the buttoning points. Then fold the right half of the material to the left just enough to reveal the bottom-centre buttoning hole on the reverse side of the material.

From the back of the chair, sew the twine through the stuffing 10mm away from the centre of the buttoning point. Pull the twine through half its length. Pass the needle through the correct hole in the top cover, and turn the folded part of the cover to face out again. Thread the needle and twine through the loop of a button, back through the hole in the material, and then out through the stuffing, 10mm on the opposite side of the centre of the buttoning point.

Tie the upholsterer's slip-knot in the twine at the back of the chair. Now cut a 50mm square of any tough material that you have to hand. Leathercloth or hessian are ideal. Roll up one square to form a small toggle, and place it under the loop you have formed in the twine. Its pur-

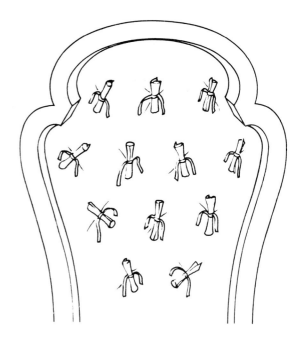

4.52 Insert a toggle of tough fabric under each twine to prevent the twine cutting into the upholstery base.

pose is to stop the twine cutting through the upholstery [4.52].

Draw the slip-knot taut, just enough to hold the toggle in place. Do not tighten it fully yet.

Go along the bottom row, working from the centre towards the two sides in turn, threading on the buttons, with the two strands of twine passing through and back through the upholstery 20mm apart, and the toggles held underneath them at the back of the panel. When you have two rows in place, lay the seat on its back and carefully arrange the pleats to be tidy, flat, and facing downwards. Follow the same procedure, using the flat of the regulator and another similar blade that you employed on the calico.

Then go on to complete the succeeding rows up the buttoned panel, arranging the pleats as you sew on each row in turn.

When you have drawn up all the twines moderately taut, with the buttons held in place on the front and the toggles on the back, stand the chair upright and start drawing them tight. Do this gradually, working from the centre and round the panel, pulling each button twine slightly tighter each time. This will help to prevent any buttons pulling the stuffing out of shape. When you have them all quite tight, lock the slip-knots with a couple of half-hitches on top, and cut off the spare twine 50mm from the knot.

Fixing the edges

Now you can deal with the material round the edges of the buttoned area.

You may find it a simple matter to fold the pleats over exactly as you did on the calico and tack the cover in place along the relevant tacking rail. On some chairs there will be no pleats at the sides, and the material is simply drawn over the stuffing, smoothed into place and tacked down. Use temporary tacks all round until you are satisfied, then tack home. Remember to use 'fine' tacks of the smallest useable length for final coverings.

When working on some styles of chair, for example a Victorian deep-buttoned spoonback, you will need to finish your material in a rebated channel. First finish the calico neatly just short of the rebate corner. On this style of chair you can afford to underturn the calico edge to ensure that no stray threads creep out to spoil the final appearance.

Bring the cover over the upholstery edge, turn it under, and hold it in place with skewers. Go all round the chair skewering the material until you have a perfect fit. On surfaces that are more or less straight and square, you will have no difficulty in determining where the pleats should lie. But on this kind of Victorian furniture the shapes can be extremely irregular. Generally, pleats will look best if they meet the nearest part of the frame at an approximate right-angle. But you might find the material falls into more comfortable pleats at different angles in some places. Use your judgement.

When you have positioned the pleats and flattened them out with the two regulator system, tack them down all round. Push the material well into the corner of the rebate with your regulator.

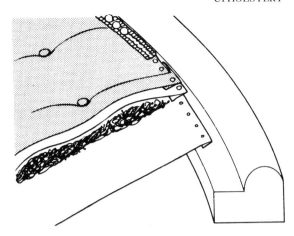

4.53 Typical stuffing sequence for a show-wood chair comprises hessian, hair, calico, top cover and gimp, all tacked on to the same rebate.

Tack home between the pleats. Take great care when tacking to ensure that you do not hammer the surrounding frame. This is 'show' wood and it will be extremely difficult to repair any damage once the upholstery is in position. Using a small-headed cabriole hammer, with the head wrapped firmly in a duster, might help.

On show-wood chairs you will have to apply a decorative trim to cover the exposed edges of the material. You can use either gimp or braid. Glue it in place with PVA adhesive and/or stitch it for complete safety. Be extremely careful with the adhesive. The slightest spillage at this stage will be difficult to remove from the cover fabric. Alternatively, you can fix it with gimp pins, which are small tacks painted to match most colours of fabrics, so they cannot be seen [4.53].

Because of the danger of spilling adhesive, most professional upholsterers prefer to finish the back of the chair completely before they begin to cover the seat.

123

Close-nailed finish

Instead of braid, an attractive finish for edges can be achieved with decorative nails, knocked in to form a row all round the length of the rebate. It is possible to buy studs covered in fabric or leather, and you may be able to find one that matches your covering material. Usually, however, up-holsterers use brass, dome-headed nails. They are available in three finishes – polished brass, light antique and dark antique. Buy nails with solid brass heads and steel shanks. Brass-plated studs soon loose their finish.

It takes great patience, a skilled hand and a good eye to space a row of nails perfectly all round a rebate, each one sitting snugly against the shoulder of the show-wood and against its two neighbours. Experienced upholsterers can work successfully by eye, but the beginner might use-fully make up a device for indicating the position where the point should be started. A pair of dividers makes a good tool. Also, it can help if you make a pilot hole, half the length of the shank of the nail, with a fine awl or even a fine drill. This will help you hammer the nails in perpen-dicularly in the right place, and will help prevent splitting the wood with the neat line of perfora-tions which close-nailing produces.

Sprung surfaces

If you are buttoning the seat of a sprung chair, or the sprung back of a chesterfield, you will not have the ready access to the reverse side of the upholstery base that you need. Important parts of the work will therefore have to be done from the face side of the article.

You will not, for example, be able to work the slip-knot tight behind the surface. You need room to work with your hands for that. Instead take the upholstering up to the calico stage as on a webbing base. Then, instead of threading the needle and twine through from the rear to the front, stitch through from front to rear, then back. If you can skewer a toggle on to another long needle, you should be able to poke it in from the back, through the webbing and among the springs, and slip it under the loop of twine. Then you can pull the twine taut from the front, trap the toggle, and withdraw your needle.

Now, at the front of the buttoned panel, pass the two ends of twine through the hole in the covering material and one of them through the loop in the button. Tie a slip-knot and draw the twines taut enough to hold the button in place while you go on to the other buttoning points and pleats, as before. Carry out the final tightening from the front, by easing the slip-knot down into the button recess, with the button following it. Knot the two ends of the twine together against the slip-knot.

Now you can either cut off the ends of the twine close to the knot, and tuck them away under the button, or you can make a better job by threading the ends in turn on to a long double-pointed needle, and taking them down through the cover close to the button. Pull and push the needle right through the base and out at the web-bing side. The twine will pull out of the eye of the needle inside the upholstery base and lie out of the way among the springs.

Applying the calico loose

The second main variation lies in the second stuffing process.

Some upholsterers prefer to start fitting the calico, and apply the second stuffing with the cal-ico in place. Proceed as far as the scrim, and mark out the buttoning points on it, using skewers from the rear according to your first paper plan.

Now, take a steel tape measure and form it into the shape the final stuffing will take between two buttoning points. Transfer the measurement to your second paper plan. It is well worthwhile building a small sample area of deep-buttoning to these measurements to check that they are exactly what you want. Alter them if necessary, and go on to complete the paper plan for the entire surface. Cut small holes in the paper at the buttoning points and transfer them on to the cal-ico by marking through the holes.

Next, sew the calico to the seat at all the but-toning points along the bottom two rows. This will form a row of loosely hanging half-pockets, open at the top and bottom alternately.

Take small wads of stuffing, tease them out and stuff them into these half-pockets, pushing well into the corners, and building up the curving shape of a half-bun. When the pockets are well filled, you can pleat the calico along the zigzag line between the two rows of buttons.

Now sew the third row of buttoning points,

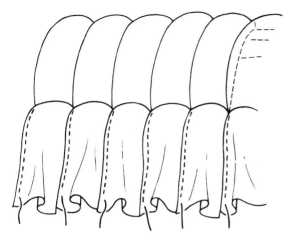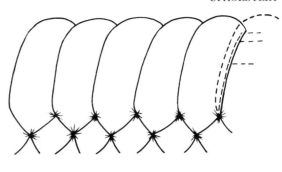

4.54 Sew a length of twine into a pleat as an aid to ensure that the pleat lies flat.

and begin stuffing the new set of half-diamonds you have formed. Work first on the alternating pockets that will complete the first row of diamonds, or they will shortly be inaccessible. Follow by working stuffing into the new half-set. Pleat between points and sew on the new rows as you go, to complete the area.

Of course, you will have now to apply the protective wadding between the calico and top cover. This is perfectly acceptable, and is in fact the procedure adopted by many upholsterers as normal practice.

Sewn channels

In some cases, simply pleating the channels at the side and edges of a panel of deep-buttoning is not enough to hold them firmly in place. This applies especially where the stuffing between the channels runs over the edge of a surface, and where it is bulbous. Also, when upholsterers use foam under the deep-buttoning, the pleats tend not to bed into the stuffing well enough to hold. The answer is to sew the pleats invisibly.

Cut a half-metre length of twine and secure one end at the buttoning point, either by knotting the end and sewing it through from the reverse side, or by knotting it round the shank of the last button before the channel.

Arrange the material into the channel, pleat it temporarily, and mark the exact bottom of the pleat with a notch. Fold the material back over the buttoning points. Now fold up the pleat again, so that the material lies right side to right side, and so that the pleat runs exactly to the mark you have made. Pull the twine up into this pleat, and sew a line of neat stitches into the pleat, 13mm below the twine [**4.54**].

Pull the material back over the stuffed area and distribute the material along the twine to take up the shape of the crowns between the channels. Tear out the stitches as far back up the channel as the edge of the frame.

Cut a small hole in the covering material so that you can pass the twine through it to the outside of the cover, and knot the twine round a tack to keep it taut.

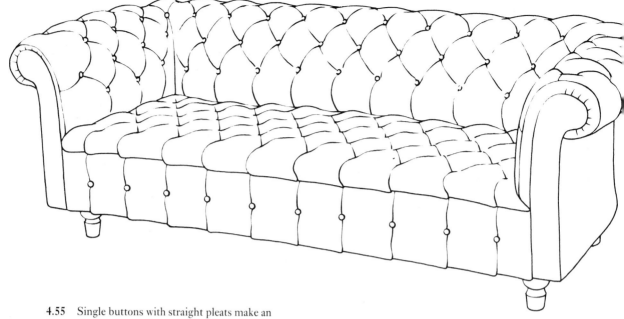

4.55 Single buttons with straight pleats make an interesting border, and complement the bulbous curves found elsewhere on a chesterfield.

Alternative buttoning patterns

Bear in mind that not all deep-buttoning patterns involve diamond shapes. The sturdy chesterfield has a front border decorated with straight pleats with a button at the centre [**4.55**].

This style can also be used to advantage on the arms of show-wood chairs, like the arm of a drawing-room chair. The pleats go across the arm and are tacked down into a rebate. Fixing the buttons in place is slightly complicated by the wood of the arm. You can deal with it either by drawing the twine to the sides and tying it out of sight round two tacks, or you can use a different kind of button, made with a nail-type shank instead of a loop. Hammer it into the wood when you are ready to tighten down the buttoning points. Protect the material from the hard face of the hammer with a duster or rag.

Omitting the calico

Having reached this point and produced some good deep-buttoning, it may be disturbing to learn that most professionals do not work like this at all. Normally, they do not bother with a calico cover, but fit the top cover material on to the top stuffing, with just a layer of wadding over it to stop the hair coming through. You may prefer to do this, but you will still find that the calico makes the whole job easier. You have some opportunity to correct your mistakes before working with the expensive fabric and you do not have to handle the cover material so much.

Many experienced upholsterers will also use a layer of 10mm thick foam instead of the felt. Foam will keep the hair from penetrating the cover, just as wadding does. In addition, it gives a smooth finish, especially when used underneath hide or leathercloth.

To accommodate the buttons, cut a clear 25mm diameter hole in the foam at each buttoning point. And be careful to keep the foam in position as you draw each of the twines taut. The foam tends to grip the covering material and is easily pulled out of place.

If you do decide to use foam, remember, as mentioned earlier, that the life of foam in furniture is unlikely to be as long as that of traditional, non-synthetic materials. It is also important to bear in mind the flammable nature of such substances and the associated risk of toxic fumes and smoke.

OTHER KINDS OF UPHOLSTERED CHAIR

Anybody who develops an interest in upholstery will soon realise that chairs and sofas cover an almost infinite variety of designs, and that only rarely can any two examples be upholstered exactly alike.

However, there are only a limited number of basic processes, and these can be learned to a level which will meet the demands of most kinds of seat. After that the upholsterer's own individual skill comes into play, to enable him or her to amend and adapt the basic processes to fit any seat he or she is working on.

Apart from restoring existing chairs to their original specifications, the experienced and confident upholsterer can enjoy the even more rewarding activity of building upholstered furniture to his or her own design, producing a completely custom-made article. Even if you do not feel competent to design your own upholstery from the bare frame, you will nevertheless have the skill and technical knowledge to build your own chairs and sofas to designs taken from elsewhere. You can study existing designs in museums, furniture showrooms, books and catalogues, and if you have followed through the basic processes, you will be able to reproduce them, or develop and amend them to meet your individual tastes.

Sprung backs
Sprung backs present no more problems than the sprung seat, but you must build them carefully because any faults in the stuffing can cause great discomfort. If the top stuffing is made smooth, using best quality hair, then the springing can produce a pleasant and luxurious support for the sitter.

Installing the springing is almost the same process as on the seat. First you must plan where the springs should fit and what gauge you plan to use.

Back springs do not carry any direct weight so they can be softer than seat springs. But remember the back should give relatively firm support, since softness can itself produce discomfort.

On a typical high-backed chair such as a wing chair, four rows of three springs makes a suitable pattern. Start the bottom row 75mm from the top

of the seat, or 175mm up if you are planning to use a seat cushion. The top row can curve gently in line with the top of the chair back, about 50mm below the rail. Position the other rows evenly in between, using your experience on the seat as a guide to achieve a good layout.

Install the webbing to suit the spring pattern. In a sprung back the webbing is fitted to the rear edges of the back posts, just as the seat webbing was fitted on the underside. The structure will be stronger if you arrange the points where the webbing strands cross so that they fall directly under the individual springs. Sew on the springs with triangular patterns of twine, then lash them with laid cord. Cover with a layer of hessian, and tack it down all round, just as on the seat.

You can now proceed through the standard upholstery steps for a sprung surface.

Secure the hessian to the springs, put in some bridles, and apply the first stuffing. Put on a scrim cover, and secure the first stuffing with through-stuffing ties. Work from the back of the chair with a long needle, and make sure that you do not snag any lower rungs of the springs.

Stuff and regulate the edges, then sew in any hard edges to give the shape you want. Sew a pattern of bridles into the scrim, and apply the second stuffing, followed by wadding and calico.

Sprung arms
Sprung arms are quite straightforward. They are appropriate on large balloon-type armchairs and settees, on which the top rail of the arm is in the form of a board or platform.

Four 100mm springs are generally enough, stapled to the board or tacked down under a strand of webbing as the front seat springs were.

The top coils of the springs are fixed in place by another strip of webbing, with the springs pulled down and sewn to it. Cover this with hessian and tie the springs to it with the usual triangles sewn on with twine.

Add through-stuffing ties, hair, wadding and calico. There is no second stuffing because in chairs of this type there is no need for a hard edge.

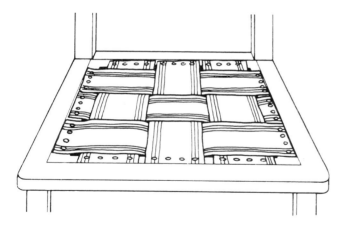

4.56 On a rebated seat frame, install the dust lining directly beneath the webbing, and tack the two together.

SMALL CHAIR WITH SEAT FITTING IN REBATED FRAME

A common type of chair has a padded seat fitted into a rebate in the top of the frame [**4.56**]. It is generally delicate, and experience on more robust upholstery is advisable before you start work on this type of chair.

You will need, in addition to the normal tools, the cabriole hammer with its small head designed for fixing tacks with less risk of damaging the show-wood of the frame.

An extra precaution is to wrap the hammer head firmly in a duster.

All layers of upholstery must fit into the rebate. So cut and fold a square of black lining to meet exactly the shoulder of the rebate. Lay it in place and fit the webbing over it, with the webbing tacks holding the black lining.

Add hessian and sew bridles into the hessian with a curved needle, taking care not to pick up the black lining in the stitches. Add stuffing, felt, calico and the cover. The cover can be left with a raw edge. Cut and fold it at the corners to give the smoothest possible fit. When you have tacked off the cover all round, finish the job with matching braid or gimp, glued and sewn all round in the rebate.

SMALL CHAIR WITH SPRUNG SEAT IN SHOW-WOOD FRAME

The combination of a sprung seat in show-wood frame occurs in many different styles and sizes of chair. A wide range of Victorian chairs are like this.

Because the bottom of the front frame member follows a pronounced curve in several directions, it is difficult to fit the normal webbing on the underside of the frame to carry springing.

Instead, fix the webbing on the top side of the frame, and install a small spring. A 75mm or 100mm spring of light gauge would be suitable, depending on the height of seat you require. A pattern of eight springs, set as in [**4.57**], would be appropriate, but you will have to use your judgement depending on the exact shape of the seat frame.

Fit the springs, sewing them to the webbing, and lashing them with laid cord. Cover with hessian and sew them in. Add bridles and the first stuffing. Cover with scrim and sew a pattern of through-stuffing ties. Cut the scrim to fit all back posts exactly as for the stuffed-over seat.

Now sew in a roll edge about 75mm high. It will take at least one row of blind stitches and two rows of top stitches.

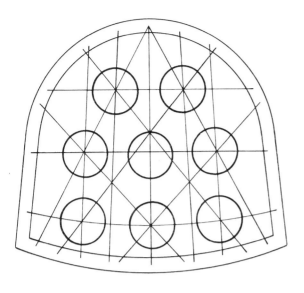

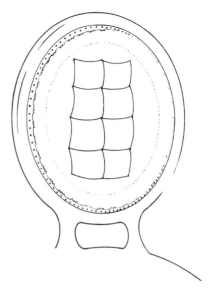

4.57 The spring and lashing pattern for a wide range of Victorian and other show-wood chairs.

4.58 Install the outside back cover first, followed by a double layer of hessian, on this type of show-wood back.

This combination – springs in the centre and a hard edge sitting directly on the frame – occurs widely. It differs from work previously described in this book because there is no complicated sprung front edge to deal with, as in the basic sprung chair.

Add bridles for a second stuffing, then wadding, calico and cover.

Bring the cover down to fit into the shoulder of the rebate at the front of the frame, smoothing it out and cutting it off to shape.

The normal trimming in a chair of this type would be gimp – glued and sewn in place. Useful alternatives are a line of close-nailing, which is especially appropriate with hide, leathercloth or velvet; also piping or double piping.

If you plan to trim with piping, fit the piping first, then add a strip of cardboard tacked in place to keep the piping securely against the show-wood. Bring the cover down to it, turn it under, and slip stitch it to the piping all round.

FRENCH-BACK CHAIR

This is the name given to certain spoon-back and medallion-back chairs. The back consists of a circular or oval open frame, with a rebate round the front. Upholstering this type of chair back involves applying the cover fabric to both the outside and inside faces of the chair back.

This chair back, like the small rebated seat which in many ways it resembles, is a delicate piece of furniture, and not recommended as a first project for the inexperienced upholsterer. The rebate may not be all that robust, and if it is not treated carefully it can be split by the various circles of tacks necessary. Use a cabriole hammer and work with the smallest possible number of tacks, of the smallest possible size consistent with a secure finish.

The outside back must be fitted first, as it is tacked to the rebate.

Temporarily tack the cover in place, right side outwards. Check that any pattern, or the grain in plain material, is straight. Start the tacking at the bottom and pull the material to the top. It is important to get the right tension. Too tight, and it will run the risk of tearing under pressure; too loose, and it will sag and look unattractive. A

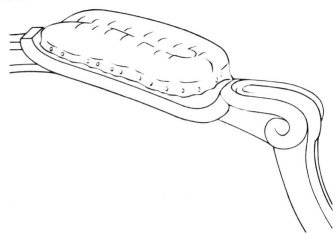

4.59 Build up the padded arms on show-wood chairs with a hard edge. The sequence is the same as on any other upholstered surface, but in miniature.

good guide is to try to pinch it between a thumb and finger. If you can pinch it up between opposite tacks, it is too loose. Smooth it out and tack at points between the top and sides, and then between the bottom and sides, and lastly at the sides.

Next, install padding to soften the outside back. A thin layer of synthetic wadding is ideal. Follow it with two layers of hessian, cut to fit inside the rebate. Webbing is not suitable for this kind of chair back; there is no space for it in the inside back, and it is difficult to stretch it over the frame. A double layer of hessian is enough to hold the stuffing in place for the inside back [**4.58**].

Tack the hessian in place in the rebate, and sew in a pattern of horizontal bridles to prevent the stuffing slipping downward when the chair is in use. Stuff it carefully. Next comes an operation which betrays the difference between quality upholstering and production-line work. The inside back should be built up proud of the wood of the frame. This gives the sitter comfort, as his or her back need not then rest on the wood. Recall the first edge sewn on the stuffed-over seat. This type of chair back employs the same techniques.

Start by picking stuffing on to the hessian, and between the lines of bridles, until you have a smooth surface. Add a cover of scrim, cut generously, and sew in through-stuffing ties with a curved needle, taking care not to let your needle catch the fabric of the outside back. Lift the edge

of the scrim all round, and tuck in best quality hair, sufficient to make a firm roll. You should have just enough room to tuck the scrim under the hair, to give a good estimate of when you have enough stuffing in place to complete the roll.

When you are ready, tack the scrim down all round the rebate. Now sew the hard edge with a row of blind stitches, followed by two rows of top stitches. You will not be able to use a double-pointed needle on the roll because the frame itself will cause an obstruction. Use a curved needle instead, and sew top stitches only.

Follow with a second stuffing of best quality hair. Add more bridles if the through-stuffing ties are too tight. Then add wadding, and the calico cover. Finally, fit the top cover, again ensuring that any pattern or grain is exactly vertical.

Because there is a roll edge sewn in the back, there should now be a pronounced valley between the upholstery and the frame, showing a row of tacks and the raw edge of the top cover material. Hide this with braid or gimp. Glue it on (carefully avoiding spillage) because it is too difficult to sew it in to this inaccessible location. Fortunately, the trim is protected by the hard edge and the frame, and it will not get the buffeting that can tear braid off more exposed parts of chairs. The extra security of sewing the braid or gimp in place is therefore not so important.

Building arms on a show-wood chair

The small padded arms of Victorian and French-style chairs [4.59] do not require any unfamiliar techniques, but they can be difficult to match each other. Being small, any irregularities show up all too clearly.

The upholstery process resembles that on the stuffed-over seat, so start by chiselling a small bevel round the edge of the top surface, on which to tack the scrim.

Put a couple of bridles along the top of the arm, held in place with tacks, and tuck some stuffing under them. Cut a cover of scrim 100mm over length and 75mm over width to allow for handling, and for the extra surface of a rolled edge.

Underturn the scrim, and adjust it and the stuffing to give a firm roll about 20mm thick when finished. Tack it all round into the bevelled edge.

To sew the roll use a medium-sized curved needle. The wood of the arms at the ends of the pad will prevent you using the double-ended needle.

Put in one row of blind stitches and a row of top stitches, and you should produce a firm dished platform overhanging the show-wood by a small margin all round. Trim off the excess scrim.

Add a layer of top stuffing and wadding to give a slightly crowned finish, and cover it with calico, tacked down round the rebate where the pad area meets the show-wood of the frame. Most professional upholsterers prefer to complete these small items up to calico-covering stage early in the process. Installing the cover is virtually the same as installing the calico. If there is a pattern, make sure it runs accurately front to back, and cut both arm covers at the same time to be sure of a perfect match. Finish with a gimp trim, close-nailing, or piping according to what suits the chair.

VICTORIAN BALLOON-BACK CHAIR

Chairs of this type, variously called Victorian balloon-back, spoon-back or nursing chairs, may well present the greatest challenge to your upholstery skills.

As in the upright chair, the main difference from factory products lies in the treatment of the edge of the upholstery, where it meets the frame on the inside back.

The basic steps for this type of chair are: sprung seat with hard edge; padded back with hard edge all round (as on the French-back chair) produced from a scrim tube (as on the wing chair); installation of a lumbar swell; deep-buttoning and trim; and padded arms.

Work on the seat as on any sprung seat with a hard edge. It may be stuffed-over at the sides, and have show-wood left at the front. On larger 'gentleman's' chairs the seat cover will require cutting round wooden arm uprights at the front. Work on the seat is, however, best left to last; the back is the interesting part. The frame will probably have an upright at the centre of the back. If so, tack three or four horizontal strands of webbing across the inside back, tacking to the centre upright at the same time to preserve the curve. Add a layer of hessian, pulled tight and tacked into the rebate all round. You will have to cut notches out of the overturn in the hessian to accommodate all the curves of this type of back.

Now recall the upholstery procedure for the wing chair. It involved sewing a strip of scrim on to the hessian to form a roll edge. This chair back is similar. Cut a strip of hessian 180mm to 200mm wide, long enough to fit right round the curves of the chair back. Draw a line accurately 75mm in from the rebate all round, either with tailor's fine chalk or a soft pencil.

Sew a row of bridles into the hessian all round the back between the rebate and the line on the hessian. Sew the scrim, with a 13mm underturn for strength, to the chalk line all round the chair. Gather it into pleats as it goes round the curves at the top, and tack it to the bottom tacking rail where it meets the bottom at each side.

Pick stuffing hair under the bridles and then arrange the scrim to form the tube. Continue to fill it, and tack it down temporarily round the rebate. Regulate the hair to produce the size, shape and firmness of stuffing you require.

Here, you will certainly have to use your own judgement to determine how much stuffing to put into this part of the chair. The key is to have a clear picture in your mind of what you are aiming for.

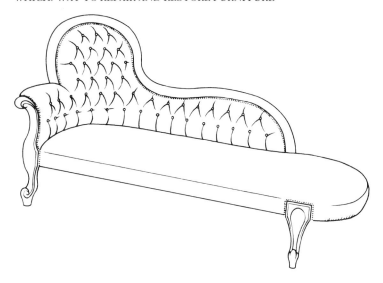

4.60 A deep-buttoned chaise-longue with sprung seat will call for a full range of skills from the most advanced upholsterer.

The idea is to build up, by stitching, a hard roll standing out about 50mm proud of the rebate, so that the upholstery clears the frame by a generous margin. The edge will be at right angles to the frame, leaving a clear, well-defined channel all round the upholstery. To work in this channel you will of course need to use a fine cabriole hammer, and you will have to take enormous care not to damage the show-wood of the frame.

Because of the problems of access, you will also have some difficulty in sewing the blind and top stitches that form the roll. A straight needle is useless; a curved needle will do the job, but they are not easy to obtain with both ends pointed, which is what you need for blind stitching. You could put a sharp end on one yourself. Otherwise, try penetrating the stuffing and scrim with the threaded end of the needle as it is. You may manage it.

Now another complication – the lumbar swell. This involves that area of the back from a point level with the arm tops down to the seat, and forms a gentle curve. It is formed from the roll edge stitched into the tube but will have to stand away from the frame more than the rest of the

scroll, to give the kind of shape you require.

So, put much more hair in the roll from the arm tops to the bottom rail. Regulate it, and insert an extra row of blind stitches and an extra row of top stitches to form a really pronounced hard edge, as much as 125 or 150mm high.

In the centre of the lumbar swell, sew a panel of scrim across the hessian between the two rolls. Fill it with a well-shaped first stuffing and tack the scrim to the bottom rail. Then put in a pattern of through-stuffing ties to prevent the stuffing falling.

You should now have the base for a well-shaped Victorian chair. And you can go on to finish the back with deep-buttoning.

The technique for deep-buttoning is standard except that in the centre of the back is a vertical rail. Run the twines on each side of it and do not bother with a toggle.

Another special consideration is to decide what pattern of buttons would suit the chair and what direction to arrange the pleats between the outer buttons and the frame.

Finish all the edges with matching gimp or close-nailing.

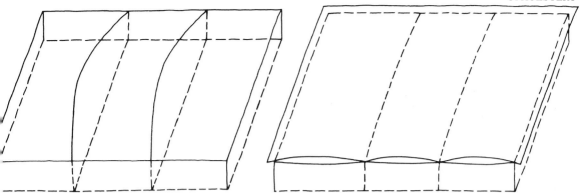

4.61 Sew partitions into the inner cushion casing, then
sew on the top cover leaving gaps for the filling.

BUILDING CUSHIONS

Cutting the cover

Although you will have fixed the general design
of your cushions even before you began upholstering a chair, you should leave making the
cushions until last. Then you can make them fit
the chair exactly, with the pattern well matched
to the chair cover.

However, bear in mind the production of the
cushion as you work on the rest of the chair.
When you come to cut the covers, check that the
area of fabric earmarked for the cushion will look
right (on the top at least). Remember also that the
cover will last longer if you can turn it over
periodically, so it is useful to have the bottom
matching, as well as the top. If this doesn't seem
possible, check the fabric for the outside back and
outside arms. It may be that you can get a better
match by interchanging one of these with the
cushion cover. And, as a last resort, if the pattern
arranged for the top cushion panel makes a
thoroughly bad match with the rest of the chair,
try switching fabric earmarked for the outside
back to the cushion top, and using a different –
but compatible – fabric on the outside back.

The inner casing

An inner casing for the cushion stops the filling
penetrating the cover. Down in particular needs a
specially coated ticking. Do not crease down-
proof ticking or the coating may be broken and
the filling may penetrate.

Make the inner casing 25mm bigger than the
outer cover, in its length and width. This will
make it fill out the cover completely and help to
preserve a good firm shape.

Large cushions, and cushions for the back of a
seat (generally called pillows) should have partitions built into them to stop the filling shifting.

Cut out the top and bottom, and the border, of
the inner casings, using the same template as for
the cover, but with the 25mm increase.

Measure and cut the partitions. They should
be between 150mm and 225mm apart, so the
length of the cushion will determine how many
you have. They are shaped to preserve the fullness of the cushion, rising to a crown. Make them
the same height as the border at the ends, rising
to twice the height of the border 150mm in from
the cushion sides. The plan for cushions and
their partitions is illustrated in [**4.61**].

Sew the border to one cover all round. You can
leave the seam allowance showing. Do not
attempt to turn a down-proof ticking casing
inside out or you will crack the coating. Sew in
the partitions along the bottom of the 'box' you
have formed, and at the sides. Sew the top to the
partitions and to the border, except along one
side of the cushion. This will leave an opening for
filling each compartment.

Now fill the cushion. Begin by taking up the
filling carefully by the handful and pushing it
into the back corner of each partition, working in
rotation to keep them balanced. When the
cushion is almost full, add more to the centre
pocket or pockets because they are cut fuller than
the end ones.

133

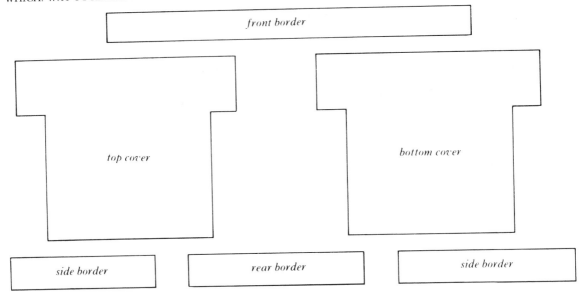

4.62 Parts for the cover of a typical T-shaped cushion.

Be careful in handling the filling material, especially if it is down. Not only is it too expensive to waste, but any form of feather filling is easily blown about a room and is extremely difficult to clean up.

Finally, sew the gaps in the ticking to close the pockets completely. Give the casing a good pummelling to distribute the feathers evenly.

Now all you have to do is insert the filled inner casing into the outer cover. The seams of the inner cushion will remain on the outside, but should not cause any problems.

Making the cover

How you treat the cushion depends to a great extent on your choice of filling. All good quality cushions should have an inner and an outer case. The inner case will be made of down-proof ticking for a feather filling; hair-proof ticking for hair filling; and ticking of any kind, or calico, for kapok.

Casings made of close-weave materials can make a loud noise when somebody sits on them, or can be uncomfortably hard. So, install a breather-vent to let the air out freely. Small vents are available for sewing into the material. Alternatively, include a panel of some open-weave material like denim, in an unobtrusive part of the cushion such as the rear border.

The best way to cut the cover is to make a template of the chair seat. Lay a piece of brown paper on the seat itself. Hold a soft pencil or blue crayon vertically against the sides and back, and scribe a mark along the line where the sides and back join the seat. If the sides and back have been upholstered correctly, they should be vertical at these points to give support to the cushion.

Next, lay a heavy book on the seat so that it lines up with the front edge and fold the paper up against the edge of the book. Rub the pencil or chalk along the angle to indicate the front of the cushion on the template. It will leave a rough line. Smooth out the line and push skewers through it to show on the top side of the template. Join up the holes, and cut round the line with a 50mm margin to complete the template.

Fold the template down the middle. The two sides should match. If they do not (and this is more often the case than not) then trim one or mark the other for over-cutting to achieve a compromise. If the disparity is too great you may not be able to eliminate it and you will have to accept that the cushion will fit only one way up.

When you are ready to cut the top and bottom of the cushion cover, lay the template on the fabric. Make sure it is square to the weave and the pattern, and that the design falls just where you want it. Mark round the template, adding 20mm

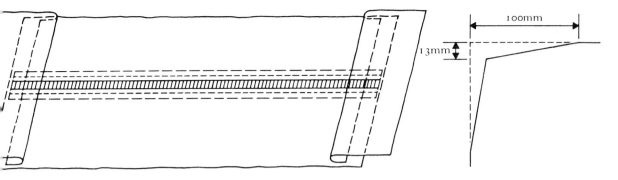

4.63a Sew the zip into separate half widths of the border. Then sew the zipped section into the rest of the border.

b Trim the corners to avoid long points which might overhang the seat.

seam allowance all round. Lay the top cover panel over the remaining fabric, wrong sides together, and use it as a template to cut the bottom panel.

Finally cut the borders of the cover. The width should be equal to the depth of cushion you require. The length is the distance round the cushion to be joined at the sides and back. Make sure you have enough piping made up to outline the top and bottom of the cushion [4.62].

First sew the piping to the top and bottom covers all round using a sewing-machine. Cut a notch into the corners so that the piping can turn the corner cleanly. Where the piping joins, take the material from the machine and peel back the piping cover. Cut the cord to form a butt joint end to end. Underturn one end of the fabric, slot the other under it, and sew a neat obliquely angled join as flat as possible.

Take up the pieces for the border, and check to make sure that any design falls correctly in the centre of the front border, and that it corresponds as well as possible with the design on the top cushion panel. Sew the border pieces end to end, without a seam occurring on the front of the cushion.

Before you sew the border to the top and bottom, plan to incorporate the opening through which you will insert the filling when the cover is completed. The traditional method is to close the

cover finally with a slip stitch. Modern practice is to close it with a zip. The zip gives access to the filling at a later date for any adjustments.

Washing or cleaning the cover of the cushion is not advisable. It will never again match the rest of the chair cover, which you cannot wash.

If you want to close the cushion with a zip, buy one specially made for upholstery. Zips made for clothing are not strong enough. Arrange the zip to fit in the centre of the rear border.

Cut the panel into two lengthways to accommodate the zip, and sew one part of the zip to each side. Sew the ends to the border [4.63a].

Before you start assembling the cover, cut a small triangle off each side of each corner, 100mm × 13mm. This allows for the 'crown' of the cushion, and gives the corners a neatly rounded look. If this trim were not made, the cushions would develop a slightly acute angle at the corners and form a weak point [4.63b].

Sew the border to the top cover. Align the pattern exactly, and pin the seam allowance on each part together. Start sewing at the centre, and sew towards each corner, then along the sides. Go all round the top cover.

The difficulty starts when you come to the bottom panel. If it is not incorporated accurately, the entire cushion will warp and wrinkle. Start by marking the centre of the bottom panel front edge with a pin or a small notch. On fabric covers, you can follow a thread across the border fabric to give you the exact centre of that. Pin the two centres together for sewing.

On materials such as hide or leathercloth, there will be no thread to follow. Instead, fold the border material in half lengthwise, and align the two edges. Mark the bottom centre to correspond with the top centre, and unfold the border. Do the same at the corners to make sure they align accurately. Continue sewing the bottom cover to the border until you have just enough left to fit the filling into the casing comfortably.

For what is to be a down-filled or kapok-filled cushion, leave a gap of about 250mm to be sewn after filling. If you are inserting a slab of foam rubber, do not sew it more than 50mm beyond the front corners, leaving almost three complete sides open to work the cover on to the foam. Of course, on a cover with a zip there will be no need for such an opening.

Foam pads

There is less objection to using foam rubber as the filling for a cushion than to employing it in the upholstery of the chair itself.

Any deterioration will matter less. It is a simple operation to unfasten the cover of a cushion and insert a new piece of foam after a few years, whereas it would be highly inconvenient to have to re-upholster the chair itself.

Foam, generally a form of polyurethane, can be hard to sit on when used by itself. It is also liable to compress in use and not return to its original shape. The answer is to use a pad of wadding or linter's felt on the top of the cushion, or on both sides if the cushion is intended to be reversible.

If you are using wadding round the foam, you might find it useful to encase the wadding in a pocket of calico to reproduce the feeling of traditional upholstery on the other areas of the chair. You should sew the calico-encased pad to the foam to prevent it from moving in use.

First, prepare the foam for sewing, or the stitches will pull right through it. Cut strips of calico 75mm wide to fit along the edges of the foam block. Apply an impact adhesive to both the calico and the foam, and when it is dry, smooth the calico firmly on to the foam. You can then sew

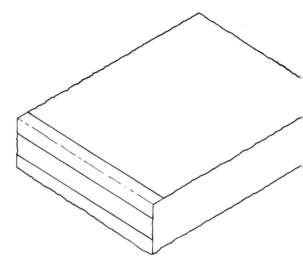

4.64 A foam-filled cushion will need strips of fabric glued to the edges. The top cover can then be sewn in place.

the calico pad to the calico edge on the foam.

Use this technique when fitting the cover to a foam pad. It helps to preserve the shape of the cushion if the cover is not able to slide on the foam. A cover should turn inside out for fitting, like a sock. Before you roll it on, sew the front edge to a calico strip along the front edge of the pad, using small stitches close to the piping [**4.64**]. Adjust the flat seam allowances of the piping seams to lie vertically down the sides of the foam block, rather than horizontally, to encourage the piping to stand up sharply.

You can also adjust the shape of a foam pad. It is sold in various thicknesses, and you can build up exactly the thickness you want by bonding two or more slabs together. You can also cut the foam to shape, using a light saw with short rapid strokes. A bread saw works well.

You can produce rounded edges by drawing together the two outer edges of a square-shaped slab, and bonding them with an impact adhesive.

When you have completed the foam filling, with the calico strips glued to it, the calico-encased pad sewn to that, and the front border of the cover also sewn to the calico strip, roll on the cover and zip up or sew the opening.

Your upholstered article is then finished.

When deciding to use foam pads for cushions, it is important to bear in mind the inflammable nature of such substances and the associated risk of toxic fumes and smoke.

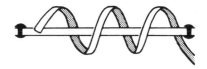

4.65   A neat taut twist will hold two lengths of cane firmly together on the underside of the frame.

CANE SEATS

Caning may look like one of the most impenetrable mysteries of all restoration work, but is in fact relatively simple. Apart from the cane itself, you will need hardly any special materials or tools.

Make up half a dozen small tapered pegs, known as 'doublers', to hold the cane in the holes while you work. 50mm lengths of thin dowel, golf tees, or fibre wall plugs do this job well.

First, carry out all the necessary structural repairs to your chair. Cut away all the old cane, and clear out the caning holes with a bradawl or drill bit of the same diameter. Drill out any stubborn pegs completely. Stain and polish the chair to the required finish. Caning is the last operation on a chair.

There are several complicated patterns that might interest advanced chair caners with unusually shaped chair frames, but the traditional standard pattern known as the seven-step or seven-stage pattern will suit most chairs.

To seat the average chair you will need about 50g of cane. The cane used in seating is a split strand with one hard glossy surface, which comes in six sizes. The finest is no 1, and is used only on delicate small chairs. For the average household chair, try to obtain approximately equal supplies of nos 2 and 4. If you are caning only one or two chairs this would mean buying a lot of surplus cane, so compromise with one gauge only, no 3.

As you work, soften the cane by running it quickly through a bowl of hot water, or moisten your finger and rub it along the flat underside of the cane only. Soaking the cane in hot water will discolour it.

Stage 1 The first strand of cane runs from front to back. You can start at a corner and work directly across the seat, or at the centre and work outwards. Starting at the centre helps if the chair is not exactly rectangular. When you reach the sides you can thread the cane into any hole that keeps the strands parallel. Measure to establish the centre at the back and front, and start your first strand either at the centre hole, or if there is no centre hole, then at the hole immediately to the left of centre. If you are working directly across the seat, start at the hole nearest to the corner that will allow the cane to lie clear of the frame.

Thread one end of the length of cane down through the hole to protrude by about 100mm. Put in a doubler to peg that end of the cane in place, then bring the other end across the seat to the corresponding hole. Thread it down through that hole, along to the next hole, back up through the frame, and across the seat again.

As you pass the cane through the holes and along the frame, turn it to make sure that the glossy surface remains on top throughout. Do not twist the cane.

Peg the cane where it comes up through each hole, to hold the strands in place without stretching or slackening. Except where you need to peg the end of a length, move the pegs along as you go, holding the cane in the most recently threaded hole.

Make the cane for this stage tense but not overtaut. The later stages will pull it tighter.

When you come to the end of a length of cane, start the new length beneath the frame. Secure it by looping it twice round the preceding strand at a point where it lies firmly stretched between two holes.

The tension in the loop will be enough to hold the new length in place [**4.65**].

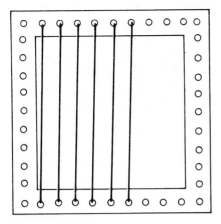

4.66 The sequence of seven strands of cane across the frame produces an attractive and reliable seat.

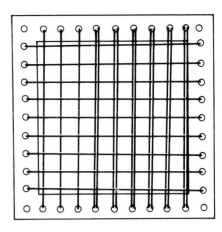

4.67

Continue working the cane back and forth along the seat until the frame is covered [**4.66**].

Stage 2 is a similar process. Work a single strand across the chair from side to side, so that the cane lies *over* the strands laid in stage 1.

Stage 3 is also straightforward. Go back to the same holes as in stage 1, and work a second strand from front to back. These should lie over the strands in stage 2, and neatly to the sides of those in stage 1. Arrange your starting point so that the cane underneath the frame occupies the spaces left vacant in stage 1 [**4.67**].

Stage 4 is the first stage that involves any weaving. The strands for this will run from side to side, and viewed from above should lie neatly to the side of those in stage 2. But they must run under all the strands in stage 1, and over all the strands in stage 3. They will lie in opposition to the strands next to them, and thereby produce a taut woven effect [**4.68**].

You can work the cane for stage 4 through the pattern with your fingers, but it is much simpler if you have a tool of some kind. The right tool for the job is a spoon bodkin. Thread it through the work to pick up about four of the strands under which the weaver will pass. Then grip the end of the cane in the spoon with your thumb, and pull it through. If the proper tool is not available, make a substitute with a length of wire bent into a

hook at the end.

Stage 5 is the first of the diagonal strands. It should be made with the thicker of your two gauges.

Start at the rear left-hand corner of the seat, and thread the cane through the corner hole. Peg it there. You may find that these corner holes are blind and do not go right through the frame. If so, double the end of the cane over before inserting it into the hole, and make up a wooden peg big enough to jam the cane in. Later, trim off the peg flush with the frame.

Start weaving the free end of the cane diagonally across the chair, passing it under the vertical pairs of strands, and over the horizontal pairs. Pass the end down the hole where it meets the frame on the opposite side. On a square chair it will be the corner hole.

You will find that you have to use the corner holes for two adjacent strands. Continue working across the chair until you have completed that set of diagonals [**4.69**].

Stage 6 consists of the opposite set of diagonals. Start at the rear right-hand corner hole, and thread the cane under the horizontals and over the verticals. You will also be going under and over the preceding set of diagonal strands. Keep checking the pattern as you go. If it has gone wrong, the only way to correct matters is to

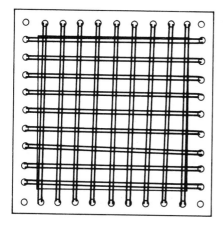

4.68

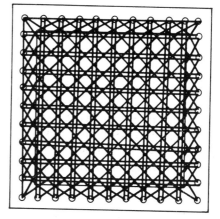

4.69

unweave all the incorrectly placed strands [**4.70**].

The pattern should now form a firm even structure, held in place by several pegs. Turn the chair over and secure all the ends, if you did not do so during the earlier stages. To do this, first trim the end of each strand to a point with a sharp knife. Moisten the cane to make it flexible, then loop it two or three times under a secure part of the cane. The bodkin or wire will also help with this awkward job. Finally hammer the twist flat, and trim the ends off close. Remove the pegs.

Stage 7 consists of laying a length of cane to form a beading that will cover the holes. It is not essential, but it gives the chair a neatly finished appearance.

If you are prepared to buy another gauge of cane, the correct type is no 6 beading cane. You will then need some no 2 to 'couch' it with. If the holes are very narrow or close together, or if you wish to economise, use no 4 cane for both parts of the beading operation.

Trim the beading cane to a point and insert it into a corner hole. Bend it over and lay it along the line of holes in the frame. Trim some of the thinner cane to a point, and pass it down through the frame one hole along from the corner. Secure it on the underside of the frame. Pass the other end over the beading cane, and back down through the same hole.

4.70

Take the thinner cane along the underside of the frame to the next hole. Pass it up through the frame, over the beading cane, and down through the same hole. Stop at the hole next to the corner hole, and secure it under the frame.

Pass another length of beading cane down through that same corner hole, and bend it along the next side of the chair. Secure the end of the thinner cane below the second hole, and pass it over the beading cane and back down through the hole.

Continue working, beading each side of the frame separately. Finally, turn over the frame and check that all the ends are neatly trimmed and hammered flat.

Suppliers

Brass and other metals

Romanys
52–56 Camden High Street
London NW1 0LT
071-387 2579

J Smith & Sons Ltd
42–56 Tottenham Court Road
London NW1 4BZ
071-253 1277

Brass fittings

J & D Beardmore & Co Ltd
3–4 Percy Street
London W1P 0EJ
071-637 7041

John Harwood & Co
28 Fairfield
Bromley Cross
Bolton
Lancashire BL7 9EE
(0204) 53089
Mail order only

J Shiner & Sons Ltd
8 Windmill Street
London W1P 1HF
071-636 0740

Woodfit Ltd
Kem Mill
Whittle-le-Woods
Chorley
Lancashire PR6 7EA
(02572) 66421

Cane

Dryad Ltd
Handicrafts Shop
178 Kensington High Street
London W8 7RG
071-937 5370

Smit & Co Ltd
99 Walnut Tree Close
Guildford
Surrey GU1 4UQ
(0483) 33113

Furniture restoration

Fitz-Glynn & Hunter Ltd
33a Clerkenwell Green
London EC1M 5RN
071-490 1055
Upholstery specialists

Alan Waterhouse and
Philippa Barstow
Unit F2
Newton Business Park
Talbot Road
Newton
Hyde
Cheshire SK14 4UQ
(0625) 616737
also French polishing

Glue and glue-pots

J Hewit & Sons Ltd
Unit 28
Metro Centre
Britannia Way
London NW10 7PR
081-965 5377

Hardwoods

J & S Agate
Maitlands
Faygate Lane
Faygate
Horsham
West Sussex RH12 4SJ
(0293) 851482

S J Atkins & Cripps Ltd
95 London Road
Bishop's Stortford
Hertfordshire CM23 3DU
(0279) 652121

John Boddy's Fine Wood
and Tool Store
Riverside Sawmills
Boroughbridge
North Yorkshire YO5 9LJ
(0423) 322370

Fitchett & Wollacott Ltd
Willow Road
Lenton Lane
Nottingham NG7 2PR
(0602) 700691

Malden Timber Ltd
Timber Mill Way
Gauden Road
London SW4 6LY
071-720 9494

Moss & Co
(Hammersmith) Ltd
104 King Street
London W6 0QW
081-748 8251

North Heigham Saw Mills
Paddock Street
Norwich
Norfolk NR2 4TW
(0603) 622979

John Thompson & Co Ltd
Hendon Lodge Saw Mill
Sunderland
Tyne and Wear SR1 2PA
091-514 4663

Henry Venables Ltd
Doxey Road
Stafford ST16 2EN
(0785) 59131

Leather and hides

Connolly Bros (Curriers) Ltd
Wandle Bank
London SW19 1DW
081-542 5251

J Hewit & Sons Ltd
(*see Glue and glue-pots*)

Leather table linings

Artisan Products
4 The Parade
Valley Drive
Brighton
East Sussex BN1 5FQ
(0273) 557418

J Crisp & Sons Ltd
48 Roderick Road
Hampstead
London NW3 2NL
081-340 0668

Woolnough Ltd
Units W107 and W110
First floor
Holywell Centre
1 Phipp Street
London EC2A 4PS
071-739 6603

Mouldings

General Woodwork
Supplies Ltd
76–80 Stoke Newington
High Street
London N16 5BR
071-254 6052

Highfield Timber Ltd
Highfield House
Hall Road
Heybridge
Maldon
Essex CM9 7NF
(0621) 856766

Winther Browne & Co Ltd
Eley's Industrial Estate
Nobel Road
London N18 3DX
081-803 3434

Polishes and stains

Fiddes & Son Ltd
Florence Works
Brindley Road
Cardiff
South Glamorgan CF1 7TX
(0222) 340323

W S Jenkins & Co Ltd
Jeco Works
Tariff Road
London N17 0EN
081-808 2336

John Myland Ltd
80 Norwood High Street
London SE27 9NW
081-670 9161

Rustins Ltd
Waterloo Road
Cricklewood
London NW2 7TX
081-450 4666

Tools

Buck & Hickman Ltd
Bank House
100 Queen Street
Sheffield
South Yorkshire S1 2DW
(0742) 766660

Buck & Ryan Ltd
101 Tottenham Court Road
London W1P 0DY
071-636 7475

Robert Sorby & Sons Ltd
Athol Road
Woodseats Road
Sheffield
South Yorkshire S8 0TA
(0742) 554231

The Tool Shop
1–3 Eagle Street
Ipswich
Suffolk IP4 1JA
(0473) 232473

Cecil W Tyzack Ltd
79–81 Kingsland Road
London E2 8AG
071-739 7126

Parry Tyzack
329 Old Street
London EC1V 9LQ
071-739 9422

Veneers, stringing and banding

Art Veneer Co Ltd
Industrial Estate
Mildenhall
Suffolk IP28 7AY
(0638) 712550

J Crispin & Sons
92–96 Curtain Road
London EC2A 3AA
071-739 4857

Index

'ff' indicates numerous subsequent references

ACKNOWLEDGMENTS

Front cover   John Parker, London.
Converted Sussex granary, courtesy of Lindsay Burtenshaw

I   (*top left*) John Parker (*top right*) Private Collection/Bridgeman Art Library (*bottom*) Haslam and Whiteway Ltd/Bridgeman Art Library; II   John Parker; III   (*top left*) Michael Stephenson Publishing (*top right*) Cotehele House, Cornwall/Bridgeman Art Library (*bottom left*) Alan Waterhouse & Philippa Barstow, Hyde, Cheshire; IV   (*top left and right*) Robin Beckham (*bottom left*) Sir Gordon and Lady Russell (*bottom right*) Alan Waterhouse & Philippa Barstow; V   Roncraft, Churchfield, Barnsley, South Yorks; VI   Fitz-Glynn & Hunter, London; VII   Fitz-Glynn & Hunter; VIII   (*top and bottom left*) Fitz-Glynn & Hunter (*right*) Private Collection/Bridgeman Art Library; IX   Boys Syndication, Woodbridge, Suffolk; X   Jaycee Furniture Ltd, Brighton, East Sussex; XI   (*top left and bottom right*) Interior Selection (*top right*) Charles Hammond Fabrics, both of Coryton Destere Ltd, London; XII   Carlysle Collection, Arthur Sanderson and Sons Ltd, London.